# MASTERING THE MBE

## Test-Taking Strategies for Scoring High on the Multistate Bar Exam

### John J. Talamo
*Attorney at Law*

SPHINX® PUBLISHING
AN IMPRINT OF SOURCEBOOKS, INC.®
NAPERVILLE, ILLINOIS

First Edition, 2002

Published by: **Sphinx® Publishing, An Imprint of Sourcebooks, Inc.®**

<u>Naperville Office</u>
P.O. Box 4410
Naperville, Illinois 60567-4410
630-961-3900
Fax: 630-961-2168
http://www.sourcebooks.com
http://www.sphinxlegal.com

This publication is designed to provide accurate and authoritative information in regard to the subject matter covered. It is sold with the understanding that the publisher is not engaged in rendering legal, accounting, or other professional service. If legal advice or other expert assistance is required, the services of a competent professional person should be sought.

*From a Declaration of Principles Jointly Adopted by a Committee of the*
*American Bar Association and a Committee of Publishers and Associations*

## Library of Congress Cataloging-in-Publication Data
Talamo, John.
  Mastering the MBE : test-taking strategies for scoring high on the multistate bar exam / John J. Talamo.--1st ed.
      p. cm.-- (Legal survival guides)
  Includes index.
  ISBN 1-57248-220-6 (alk. paper)
  1. Bar examinations--United States--Popular works. 2. Law examinations--United States--Popular works. I. Title. II. Series.

KF303 .T35 2002
349.73'076--dc21

2002017578

Printed and bound in the United States of America.

VHG Paperback — 10 9 8 7 6 5 4 3 2 1

# CONTENTS

# ABOUT THE BOOK

The title of this book was deliberately chosen to draw the analogy between the Multistate Bar Exam and learning to play a musical instrument.

There's an old joke about a tourist in New York trying to find Carnegie Hall. The tourist stops an old man on the street to ask directions. "How do I get to Carnegie Hall?" the tourist asks. The old man answers, "Practice! Practice!"

Just as you can never master the piano, for example, by studying sheet music, you will never master the Multistate by studying only the law. The law is the sheet music. The test is the piano. Once you truly understand the concept, you can become the "Maestro" of the Multistate.

This book is based on the theory that most people who fail the bar exam do so because they do not properly prepare for the Multistate portion. This is not surprising since there are few, if any, multiple-choice tests given in law school. The IRAC (Issues, Rules, Analysis, Conclusion) method for writing essays worked in law school and works on the bar exam. There is no method for multiple-choice questions and little time after graduation to perfect one.

My own survey of people in California who failed the exam at least once not only confirmed this theory but showed that those who failed the exam more than once were able to improve on other parts of the test. They could not, however, improve on the Multistate portion, even though they practiced thousands of sample questions. The reason that I attribute to this is that they kept learning more law but never learned how to do multiple-choice questions.

The person who can devote full time to studying for the bar has a huge advantage over the person who has work and family obligations. The reason is that the one who studies full time can learn how to do multiple-choice questions just by doing them. Some people do as many as three to four thousand practice questions. They get good at it without studying properly just by the sheer volume of questions that they attempt to answer. As noted above, even doing thousands of practice questions does not work for everyone.

The object of this book is to give you an efficient and deliberate way to get good at answering the type of multiple-choice questions that you will encounter on the exam. This will enable you to compete with those who have more time to study. If you have lots of time, you can use it to prepare for the essay portion or, in some states, those endless performance questions. Either way, you can use the Multistate to boost your overall score rather than trying, as many do, to overcome the poor Multistate score with brilliant essays.

Every effort has been made to keep the book short and simple. The last thing you need is one more book to study. All the books to study have been written. This book will show you how to use them more effectively.

# MATERIALS

In order to use this book effectively, there are materials you will need and rules you must follow. If you are taking a bar review course, you have been given a book containing several hundred multiple-choice questions with sample answers. The answer section not only states the correct answer, but also analyzes all the choices. In other words, it tells you why the right answer is right and the wrong answers are wrong. You must have such a book in order to study properly.

The National Conference of Bar Examiners (the people who prepare the test) offer such a book. They also offer books with the answers stated by the correct letter only, without analysis. The book with analysis is a study book. Books without analysis are practice books.

One of the major flaws for those who do poorly on the exam is to confuse study with practice. When you study, you learn. When you practice, you see how much you have learned to that point in time. Those who use the sample questions for practice only (most do), learn very little. They then wonder how they did so poorly after all those practice tests they took.

This book *does not* contain a complete set of sample questions and answers. As stated above, most of you already have a book that does. You should have this book with you at all times for reference. Use it in conjunction with your other books.

# THE RULES

Once you have the materials, you must use them properly. There are rules you must follow, which distinguish the methods in this book from those commonly used. The first rule, as indicated above, is to distinguish between study and practice. Most people study from outlines and then do 20 or more practice questions. They are careful to time their practice work. They then check their score, briefly look over the sample answers for the ones they got wrong and go back to the outline.

The time spent taking the practice test was wasted. They did not learn anything. Many of them could try those same practice questions a few days later and still get some wrong.

Their first mistake was timing themselves. It is true that you get only 1.8 minutes per question on average, but finishing on time is not difficult. Many people finish on time and still fail. You will learn how to finish with time to spare without compromising the quality of your answers.

Suppose you studied part of your outline with a timer. It did not matter how much you remembered as long as you finished on time. Then you studied another part very carefully, taking the time to really learn the material. How fast could you go through the outline a second time? The part you studied carefully would be easy. You could breeze through it quickly. The part you raced through would take much longer. The material would not seem as familiar to you.

Racing through the Multistate sample questions is even worse. These questions are the closest material to the real exam that you have. They are much closer than an outline. The difference is that you may learn the law from the outline, but you cannot learn the test. Most people know the law. They do poorly because they never learn the test.

You will learn how to study the sample questions. They will become your favorite and most valuable study method.

# READ THIS BOOK FIRST

This book should be read in its entirety before you begin to use the study methods. This will give you an understanding of the complete preparation package. This is not just a book of exercises. It is critical that you study with confidence and with proper organization to overcome the difficulties of learning the law, learning the test, and dealing with the pressures that come with taking a test that will determine your future.

The following chapters will explain:
- how the bar exam is given in different jurisdictions;
- the importance of a bar review course;

- techniques for reading and answering questions quickly but without rushing;
- exercises to improve your knowledge of the law and the test;
- special exercises if you are still having problems; and,
- the best approach to each subject.

Although the focus is on the Multistate, there is a chapter on writing essays and one on the Performance section of the test used in some states. The ending chapters deal with the pressures connected with the exam and give additional sample questions.

This comprehensive approach will give you an enormous advantage over those who simply study the law and practice Multistate sample questions.

# THE BAR EXAM 1

The bar exam is probably unlike any other test you have taken. No matter what state you are in, there are specific areas of law you must know, and different ways in which the law is tested.

## ESSAY AND PERFORMANCE

The bar exam is different depending on the state. Currently 14 states are using the Multistate Essay Examination and 21 states are using the Multistate Performance Test. These are shown in a chart in Appendix B on pages 140-141. These tests will be addressed in a later chapter.

## MBE

The Multistate Bar Examination (the multiple choice exam) is given by the District of Columbia and all states except Louisiana and Washington.

The Multistate test is given as two separate tests on the same day with a lunch break between each session. Each test consists of 100 multiple-choice questions.

You are given a question booklet containing the questions, and you may write notes in this booklet. You have a separate, Scantron-type answer sheet on which you mark your answers. The examiners will specify the type of writing instrument you must use (a number 2 pencil is currently required).

# TIME FACTOR

Each session (100 questions) must be completed in 3 hours. This means that you have an average time of 1.8 minutes per question. *Any questions not answered are treated as wrong.* This is why there is a great emphasis on finishing.

Your bar reviewer may advise you to keep track of the time and start skimming questions if you are falling behind, finally just putting down anything during the last few minutes. This may be advice that is not right for you.

By the time you take the exam, you will know from your practice tests if you have a problem with the allotted time. If you do—and even if you do not—you will have a definite plan to solve the problem should it arise on the test.

You will answer the questions that you have the best chance to answer correctly. If you put down less than a thoughtful answer, it will be on a question you probably would have missed anyway.

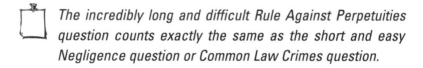 *The incredibly long and difficult Rule Against Perpetuities question counts exactly the same as the short and easy Negligence question or Common Law Crimes question.*

If you could choose which one to answer, which would you pick? The exam gives you that choice. Do not give it up. (We will cover "skipping questions" in Chapter 5.)

## THE SUBJECTS

The important thing to remember about the MBE is that it is designed to test those abilities that, in the opinion of the bar, are necessary to be an attorney. If you know enough about the law and the test, it is clear and unambiguous.

The test covers six subjects:
- constitutional law;
- contracts;
- criminal law & procedure;
- evidence;
- real property; and,
- torts.

Contracts and Torts are tested with 34 questions each; the others are each represented by 33 questions. There is no grouping of the questions by subject matter. A contract's question may be followed by a Torts question, which may be followed by an Evidence or Property question, etc. There is, however, little difficulty determining the subject matter of the question.

## THE FORMAT OF QUESTIONS

The questions on the test are asked with different formats. It is important that you familiarize yourself with each.

### Correct Choice

The first format is the obvious one where you are asked to find the correct choice. Usually the question is not worded this way.

---

## EXAMPLE:

"Which of the following would be useful as a defense"? If only one answer is useful (correct), the others are not useful (wrong).

---

## Best Answer

There is a variation of the above format that requires you to find the "best" answer. This means that more than one answer will be a correct statement of the law. The "best" answer will more specifically answer the question. A question of this type could ask you to identify which would be most useful as a defense. The difference is subtle but you must know these differences.

## Paragraph Answer

Another type is the "paragraph" answer. You are given paragraphs to read. One of them will answer the question. This is, of course, more time consuming. These questions will usually have the paragraphs first, then ask a question (which I will refer to as the "call" of the question), then the choices. It is necessary for these questions that you know the question being asked before you start reading the paragraphs. If not, you will probably have to reread them. You cannot afford the time.

Another difficulty with the paragraph question is that it may test your knowledge in several areas on one question. For example, an evidence question may ask which paragraph describes a situation where the evidence was legally (or illegally) obtained. The first paragraph may describe evidence obtained through a questionable confession, the second obtained from the search of a car after a traffic violation, the third from a possibly defective warrant, and the fourth from a hot pursuit search of a residence.

The examiners usually stay fairly close to the same type of situation but you can see the possible difficulties.

## Roman Numerals

Another is the "Roman numeral" question. You are given answers with Roman numerals before each. You must then select as your answer which combination of Roman numeral answers is correct. The correct combination may be all, some, one, or none.

For many this is the most difficult type of question. The reason is because none or more than one answer may be correct. If only one choice is correct, you pick your choice and do not worry about the others, even if you do not fully understand them. In the Roman numeral question, you must know whether each answer is right or wrong. This not only takes more knowledge but also more time.

For you it will not be difficult. The reason is that you will not only learn how to find the right choice, but you will know from your study methods which choices are wrong and why.

## Series

The "series" questions are very common on the exam. You are given a single set of facts and then more than one question about these facts. For example, the instructions will read "Questions 24-28 are based on the following facts."

There may be variations for each question. This will be indicated by telling you to "Assume for purposes of this question only," followed by the applicable change.

Sometimes the examiners will test your confidence on these questions. For example, your answer to question 24 is that no contract was formed. Question 25 starts with "Assume for purposes of this question only that a contract was formed." Did you make a mistake on question 24? Why would they instruct you to assume there was a contract if none was formed?

The answer to your concern is simply to believe what they tell you. If you are to assume something for question 25 *only*, that's what you should do. Did you make a mistake on question 24? I do not know, and neither will you. Answer all questions by marking the choice that you believe best answers the question. This is the only reason that you should ever choose an answer.

## Worst Answer

Other variations are that any of these formats may be used in a question that calls either for the wrong answer or the worst answer, such as, "which would be least helpful as a defense?"

## Because, If, or Unless

The most important and most frequent choices on the exam contain the words "because, if, or unless." This is what separates those who know the law in depth from those who have a superficial knowledge. The choice will start with either "Yes, because," "Yes if," or "Yes unless" or "No because," "No if," or "No unless." A variation could be "Win, because," "Lose because" etc. This is followed by the reason that the choice is right or wrong.

Some reasons may be incorrect statements of law. Others may be correct law but not exactly fit the facts. Others may not answer the call (the question being asked). A choice may contain more than one reason. One of the reasons may not be correct while the other reason or reasons precisely answer the question correctly. This makes it a little tougher. We will examine this later in Chapter 3.

All of these types of questions have one thing in common. They contain a set of facts. They have a call (ask a question). They have choices a, b, c, and d.

## SCORING THE TEST

Your Multistate exam score is *scaled*. This is a type of grading on a curve. The curve is based on the assigned difficulty of the exam you are taking. Your score is not like a score in school. A raw score (actual score before the curve) of 50% would probably put you close to the bottom 10% of those taking the test. However, a raw score of 70% would probably put you in the top 10% and a raw score of 80% would put you in the top 1%. This means that you can get 40 – 50 wrong and have an excellent score.

Understanding this is very important to planning your studying. It means that those areas of the law that you find most difficult can remain a mystery to you and you will still do well on the exam. This will be explained further when we set our goals in Chapter 5.

## MASTERY MARKERS

❏ I should contact the National Conference of Bar Examiners and my state bar association to find all available information and materials for my exam.

❏ I must learn the different formats used for the questions on the exam.

❏ I understand how the test is scored. This makes my studies easier since I can miss several questions in my most difficult subjects.

❏ I must know the most heavily tested areas completely and will devote my study time accordingly.

## ADDITIONAL NOTES:

# THE BAR REVIEW 2

In my opinion, a bar review course is essential to passing the exam. There are two major reasons for this: relevance and commitment.

## RELEVANCE

I will repeat the importance of studying relevant material and particularly the areas of relevant material that you have the best chance to learn completely. I will repeat it until you are tired of reading it. Unfortunately, some of you will still devote precious study time to irrelevant areas.

The amount of material that can be used for testing is well beyond the amount that can be remembered. If the examiners wanted to, they could fail almost everyone. In order to avoid this result, the examiners confine the questions to certain major areas of each subject. There are areas of the law that have never been covered on the test; other areas are rarely tested.

The bar reviewers make a meticulous study of past exams to determine where to concentrate their review. This is their job. They do it better than could you or I. Rely entirely on their judgement in this area. This is the law that you should study first. Study it until you know it heart and soul. If this takes all your Multistate study time, then this is the only law you should study. Do not worry about what may possibly be on the test. You want to know as much as you can about the areas that are most frequently tested. If you learn these areas thoroughly, you will do very well.

> *Think of it this way. If someone gave you a copy of the exam that you are going to take, would you study anything else? The closest you are going to get to this are the areas that your bar reviewers emphasize and your sample questions.*

As a result of narrowing your area of study, there may possibly be a few questions on the test that will be unfamiliar to you. Guess at an answer and move on, telling yourself that you have benefited by gaining a little extra time for those questions that require more than the 1.8 minutes. Since you are aware of this possibility, you will not panic if you come across a few of these questions. You also will not spend much time trying to figure them out. It is always possible, of course, that your guesses will be correct. That is an advantage of multiple-choice.

For example, you may not have time to thoroughly learn the Federal Rules of Evidence. However, you should be able to quote the major exceptions to the Hearsay rule. Up to 1/3 of the Evidence questions have been asked in this area. You do not have to be overly bright to figure out that you should learn that. As obvious as that appears, many will try to learn all the rules and end up not knowing the major Hearsay exceptions completely. Completely means well enough to get them all correct.

> *I will give you the relevant areas as I know them. Your bar reviewers will give you the most current areas. Rely on them, not on this book, for this information.*

## COMMITMENT

A second reason to take a bar review course is that many of us do not have the energy or discipline to go it alone. It is so easy to get distracted or be simply too tired to study. The energy of a review course will keep you focused when you would be falling asleep at home.

Never miss a lecture. You may be surprised to learn that attendance is far from perfect. This is the most important test you will take in your lifetime. What could be important enough to keep you away from your bar review?

## BAR REVIEWS AND STRATEGIES

Which bar review course should you take? I do not have any recommendations, but there are some differences between courses that you should know.

There are full and partial courses. The full courses review all sections of the test applicable to your jurisdiction. The partial ones concentrate on one aspect of the exam: Multistate, Essay, or Performance (where tested). There are those who take both a full and a partial review.

I do not know how much time, energy, and money you can devote to the bar exam. I will caution you that if you take an additional review course specifically for the Multistate, be aware that the test can be extremely difficult if you do not approach it properly. One way *not* to approach it is to get so bogged down in strategies that you forget the importance of the exam.

This is a straight forward, honest test of your ability to apply your knowledge of the law and powers of analysis by answering exactly the question that is asked. My purpose is to give you some familiarity with the test as well as study methods and exercises to get you thinking the same way the examiners think.

Once you convince yourself that this is merely a trick test, you are lost. When you let strategy dominate your thinking, you are looking for the trick instead of the choice that best answers the question asked. Since there are so many straightforward questions and so few tricks, you are not going to get many answers right. The examiners will not often try to fool you, but they do not object to your fooling yourself.

An easy way to spot this is when you need to devote study time to the strategies. You do not learn strategies. You use them to learn the test. If the strategy is so complicated that you have to use your study time to learn it, do not bother.

The correct concept is simple. In order to do well you must know the substantive law completely in those areas most heavily tested. This can be accomplished from your bar review lectures, your study outlines and, as you will see, from your Multistate sample questions. Follow the study methods and exercises you will learn in the later chapters. They will increase both your knowledge of the law and your ability to apply it to the test. Use whatever other study methods you come across that seem to produce desired results.

## Audio Tapes

Some bar reviews allow rental of tapes of the lectures. They are not available in all areas and from all bar reviews. If you have an opportunity to obtain these tapes, do so.

If you spend much time in your car, or even if you do not, audio tapes can be an enormous advantage as a study aid. I was surprised to discover that many who have them available do not use them.

This is not an easy test. Give yourself every possible chance. The everyday memory reinforcement of the audio tapes is a valuable supplement to the lectures.

The audio tapes from bar reviews are usually tapes of the prior exam's review lectures. They are similar to the current lectures. You may be tempted to substitute them for attendance at your review course. Do not do it! The combination of the current lectures and the tapes is what will give you the knowledge you need.

When you attend the lectures, you will take notes and not have the opportunity to ask questions. For these reasons, it will be difficult to remember the lecture completely. The tapes give you the chance to listen without the distraction of taking notes. Also, when questions arise, you can stop the tape and find the answer.

If you are a person who remembers what you hear better than what you read, you can almost eliminate your outlines and use them only for reference.

## TIMERS

Another word about timing yourself. Your bar review professor will most likely tell you to practice with a timer. This is good advice that does not go far enough. You should *practice* with a timer. You should not *study* with a timer. We will get to the difference later.

# MASTERY MARKERS

- ❒ I will take a bar review course if at all possible.
- ❒ I will depend on my bar reviewers to emphasize the areas most heavily tested and allocate my study time accordingly.
- ❒ I will never miss a bar review class.
- ❒ If available, I will obtain my bar review's audio tapes. I will use them to supplement the lectures but never to substitute for the lectures.
- ❒ I should not get bogged down in strategies. They tend to confuse, rather than clarify.

# ADDITIONAL NOTES:

# MULTIPLE CHOICE QUESTIONS 3

You have probably never taken a multiple-choice test like the Multistate Bar Exam. You have, of course, taken multiple-choice tests. The first thing you must realize is that if you try to answer the Multistate questions the way you answered other multiple-choice questions, you are not going to do well. The following section will tell you how to answer Multistate questions.

## FAMILIAR QUESTIONS

There are different types of multiple-choice questions. The first type is where you must know a fact. This is the kind that you are used to seeing.

---

### EXAMPLE:

The battle of Hastings was fought in
    (a) 1066
    (b) 1166
    (c) 1266
    (d) 1366

---

If you know anything about Real Property or the history of the Common Law, you know that the answer is (a). This is the type of question where you either know the answer or you don't. You cannot figure it out and you would never think that more than one choice is correct.

---

## EXAMPLE:

The leader of the French invasion of Russia in the war of 1812 was
  (a) Louis XIV
  (b) Louis XV
  (c) Louis XVI
  (d) Napoleon

---

You may not know the answer but you certainly know the question being asked. Could you figure out the answer? Possibly.

Suppose you know that Louis XVI was beheaded in 1793, following the revolution of 1789. You could reasonably guess that Louis' XIV and XV preceded Louis XVI. You also know that 1793 comes before 1812. This would eliminate all but Napoleon.

# BAR EXAM QUESTIONS

There are some questions on the Multistate that are as easy as the above examples. You know exactly what they are asking and you either know the answer or you don't. If most of the questions followed this pattern, you could study strictly from your outlines and do well. Unfortunately, most are not. The estimate by most bar reviewers is that about 20% of the questions can be answered with your law school knowledge. Another 20% are so difficult that few can answer them. The remaining 60% separate those who pass and fail. These are the questions that require knowledge of the law *and* the test.

Let's look at this type of multiple-choice question—the type most common on the test.

---

## EXAMPLE:

Don is driving his car on Main Street when he begins to get sleepy. He decides to close his eyes for a few minutes. Because he cannot see, he drives his car onto the sidewalk, hitting and injuring Paul. Paul was sitting on a bench waiting for a bus. Paul sues Don on the theory of negligence.

Paul will:

(a) Win
(b) Win, if Paul can prove that he was not contributorily negligent.
(c) Lose, because Paul should have known that this area was dangerous and, therefore, assumed the risk of being injured by Don.
(d) Win, because Don's act caused Paul's injury.

---

# ANALYSIS

This is a very easy question. It's even easier if you approach it properly. The first thing you must ask yourself is, "What is the question asking?"

This is a Tort's question. How do you approach a Tort's question? First, you determine if the Plaintiff's case proves every required element of the Tort. If not, you stop. The Plaintiff loses. If every element is there, does the Defendant have any acceptable defenses? If yes, the Defendant wins. If no, the Plaintiff wins.

We can rephrase the question to see that it is really asking if all of the elements of Negligence are given in the facts or will a choice supply a missing element? Since no defenses are presented in the facts, are there any valid defenses in the choices?

Negligence requires duty, breach of duty, causation, and damages. All are obviously contained in the given facts. There is no question as to whether Don owes a duty to Paul. Even though the question does not say that Don breached that duty, you know that deliberately closing your eyes while driving constitutes a "failure to use reasonable care." The facts state that the breach of duty (driving with his eyes closed) was the cause of Paul's injuries. Are there defenses? Let's examine the choices, starting with (b).

(b) Contributory Negligence is a possible defense. The choice is wrong for two reasons. First, it is not supported by the facts. There is nothing given to indicate any negligence on the part of Paul. However, that is not the reason you dismiss this choice. The choice asks the Plaintiff to prove that he was not contributorily negligent. Plaintiffs don't prove a lack of a defense; defendants prove defenses. Plaintiffs respond to defenses. No defense has been raised in the facts or the choice.

This is a common type of choice. The examiners don't give you choices that are close to correct. If the choice read "Unless Paul was contributorily negligent," the choice would be a correct statement of law. Even though it would not be supported by the facts, it would not directly be contradicted by the facts.

They don't make it that difficult. Every question that requires one choice to be correct will have a definite reason why the other choices are wrong. A lot of thought goes into these questions. The last thing the examiners want is to be accused of asking ambiguous questions.

(c) Assumption of Risk is a possible defense but is simply not supported by the facts. This defense requires knowledge of the risk and a decision to take the risk. It's too much of a stretch for any reasonable person to make.

That's not the only reason why it's wrong. It's wrong because it says that Paul "should have known" of the danger. Is the test for Assumption of Risk that the plaintiff *should have known* of the danger or *knew* of the danger? "Should have known" would mean Negligence, not Assumption of Risk. Again, you have two reasons to eliminate a choice.

(**d**) This choice is where you have to determine what this question is really asking. It's true that the Plaintiff must prove causation as part of a successful suit based on Negligence. The problem is that the Plaintiff must prove all four elements, not just causation. Paul will win, not because Don's act caused his injuries, but because Don breached his duty to Paul and the breach of duty caused Paul's injuries. In other words, Don's negligent act caused Paul's injuries.

The reason that this distinction is important is that in a slightly different question, based on a strict liability theory, (**d**) might be the correct answer. This is because breach of duty is not a required element for strict liability.

In this question, all of the necessary elements are contained in the facts, and (**a**) is the correct choice. This was a relatively easy question and you probably would have answered it correctly without much analysis. The point is to illustrate how much easier a question can be if you first determine what they are really asking. This analysis will be necessary for more difficult questions.

Another bit of knowledge you gained from this question is that a simple answer is sometimes correct.

*Don't dismiss the one word answer as being too simple and, therefore, probably wrong. Of course, some of the one-word answers are wrong. The reason that they're wrong is because they don't answer the question, not because they have only one word.*

## IMPORTANT CHANGES IN THE FACTS

Let's change the facts slightly and see how the choices are affected.

---

# EXAMPLE:

Don is driving down Main Street when his car veers onto the side-walk, hitting and injuring Paul who is on the bench waiting for the bus. Paul sues on a Negligence theory. Paul will:
  (a) Win
  (b) Win, if he can prove that Don was not driving with rea-sonable care.
  (c) Win, because Don caused Paul's injuries.
  (d) Lose, because Paul was not within the zone of risk.

---

Choice (d) can be easily dismissed. Many questions contain at least one "throw away" choice, and even usually come down to a decision between two of the choices.

Choice (c) is still incomplete. Causation is not disputed. It's just not enough for the Negligence theory.

Choice (a) is now incomplete. The facts do not give us breach of duty, a necessary element of Negligence. Never add facts or say to yourself, "What if?"

Choice (b) is now the correct choice. It supplies the missing element.

This is, again, an easy question if you paid close attention to the facts. It simply illustrates how the correct choice can change by slightly altering the facts. Reading every word is obviously very important.

By now you should be getting some idea of the challenge you face. There will be many choices that, to the untrained eye, appear to be correct. Many times the reason is that they contain legal points that jog your memory.

In law school you studied both Contributory Negligence and Assumption of Risk. You never studied "yes" (the correct answer in the first example). Since you are trying to relate the choice to your studies, you could pick the wrong choice because you lack the confidence to choose the unfamiliar. This is why studying outlines alone does not work. Once you study the test as well as the law, your increased confidence will allow you to pick the correct choice, familiar or not.

Before you read the study methods and exercises in this book, you will get some information on bar review courses and the bar exam in the next chapters.

## MASTERY MARKERS

❏ The multiple-choice questions on the bar exam are different from those I have seen before. It is critical to learn the test as well as the law.

❏ The precise question being asked is not always obvious. By rephrasing the question, I can clarify it.

❏ The only criterion for picking a choice is that I believe it to be correct. One-word choices should not be dismissed because they are too simple.

❏ Every word of a question may be important and cannot be skipped over. Even a slight change of the facts can change which choice is correct.

# ADDITIONAL NOTES:

# TECHNIQUES 4

A *technique* is simply a way to approach each question in order to get the maximum understanding of what is being asked and to pick a choice in the shortest amount of time. As you will see, it can be very important with certain types of questions.

## READING THE QUESTION

The most common technique for reading the questions is to:
1.  Read the call of the question.
2.  Scan the answers.
3.  Read the entire question from the beginning.

The theory is that when you read the facts, you already know what you are looking for to comply with the call of the question. A question may, for example, appear to be about Criminal Law. However, when you get to the "call of the question," it asks whether certain evidence will be admissible. Now you have to adjust your perspective. You may have to go back and reread the question. The clock is ticking.

Another example is the theory on which the suit is based. If the suit is brought based on Strict Liability, for example, you do not have to look for breach of duty in the facts or the choices. Finding breach of duty in a choice would tip you off that it is probably wrong.

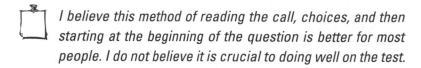 *I believe this method of reading the call, choices, and then starting at the beginning of the question is better for most people. I do not believe it is crucial to doing well on the test.*

You may find that once you become completely absorbed in the test (the practice ones as well as the real thing), you may forget this technique and simply start each question at the beginning. You will most likely have little trouble anticipating the call and the choices. Try each way and see which is more helpful, both as to the number of correct answers and the time factor.

There is one exception. Always use this technique for the "paragraph" type questions. Reading these paragraphs can be confusing if you don't know what you are trying to find. Reading the call and scanning the choices before reading the paragraphs will be helpful.

## MARKING YOUR ANSWER

Once you have decided how to read the question, you must acquire techniques to mark your answer. One that is frequently used is the True - False method. As you read each choice, decide whether it is a possibly correct answer. Mark a "T" or "F" next to the choice (you can also use "+" for possibly correct and "-" for wrong). When you have finished this procedure, you look for your marks for correct answers. If there is only one, mark that letter on your answer sheet. If there are two or more, you must decide which one is the correct choice. At least you avoid rereading the wrong choices.

This is certainly the best method for questions on which none or more than one choice may be the correct answer, and I highly recommend it for these questions. It is also very useful for the "paragraph" type questions because rereading complete paragraphs is time consuming. For the bulk of the questions—those requiring only one choice to be correct—it may be time-consuming for some of you. There are many questions where, after reading the facts and the call, you already know the answer. You are simply looking for it among the choices. You can glance at the choices and dismiss the wrong ones. For those of you who frequently find yourselves in this situation, you may want to use the True - False method only for:

- the Roman numeral type questions;
- the paragraph type questions; and,
- those questions that are more challenging for you.

Your goal is to save time without compromising your ability to answer the questions correctly. If you can combine some of these techniques to save even five seconds per question, that's 500 seconds (or over 8 minutes) per each three-hour session. However, if you are a methodical person, it makes good sense to always mark each choice and at least avoid rereading those you have dismissed as incorrect.

## MASTERY MARKERS

☐ I will practice the different techniques to see which best suit me.

☐ Once I have decided which technique to use, I will always study or practice that way.

# ADDITIONAL NOTES:

# HOW TO *STUDY* FOR THE MULTISTATE EXAM 5

As said before, studying for the MBE, and practicing the MBE are different from each other. This chapter will lay out what is entailed in *studying*.

## GOALS

Before we begin, we have to set our goals. Our first goal is to always take the easy way out. We want to concentrate least on the difficult stuff and learn the easy stuff completely. Okay, there's no easy stuff, but there are degrees of difficulty. It is certainly less difficult for most of us to learn Common Law crimes, the elements of Negligence and the major exceptions to the Hearsay Rule than it is to learn Future Interests.

This is the best thing about multiple-choice. Each question has the same value, regardless of how difficult it may be. You are not going to get them all right. Why not miss the toughest ones? These are the ones that you would probably miss anyway.

If you neglect the easier subject areas to concentrate on those really challenging areas of the law, you are going to get more wrong answers. Why? Because there are more easy areas covered than difficult ones. For every Rule Against Perpetuities question you get right, you are going to miss two or three Negligence or Contract questions that you did not study enough.

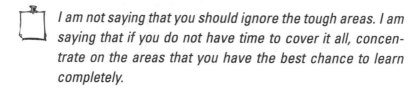

*I am not saying that you should ignore the tough areas. I am saying that if you do not have time to cover it all, concentrate on the areas that you have the best chance to learn completely.*

Rely on your bar review to pinpoint the areas most frequently tested. Then learn completely the "easy" parts of them first. Once you have done that and find that you still have time, learn the tougher areas.

Our next goal is to learn the law and the test by doing sample Multistate questions. This means that getting lots of wrong answers is, at first, a good thing.

Look at it this way, if you read your outline and learned lots of things you did not know, you would consider the time well spent. That is all you are initially trying to do with the sample questions. You are not trying to test your knowledge. You want to learn things about the law and the test. By using the following exercises, you will learn, and those using the old study methods will not.

## LEARNING THE WRONG ANSWER

You are going to find that learning wrong answers is quite different from learning right answers. It requires a much greater knowledge of the law. You'll never get this in depth knowledge from your outline or a superficial reading of your sample questions.

## TEN QUESTIONS

Begin with ten questions on any one subject. I recommend ten because this type of study is time consuming and you do not want to do more than you can remember. If you have the time, adjust the number accordingly, but take a break after each ten.

Doing ten questions will usually take about an hour. If you are going to spend four hours studying, you can do about 40 questions on one subject or study two, three or four subjects. The choice is yours. Whichever way allows you to concentrate better is the correct method.

Answer the first question. Go immediately to the sample answer. Regardless of whether you were right or wrong, read (study) the sample answer. It will explain why the correct answer is correct and also why the incorrect answers are incorrect. Always read the reasons given as to why the wrong answers are wrong, even if you knew why the correct answer was correct.

This will eventually give you the knowledge of the test (and the law) that you need, not only to get more correct answers, but to answer the questions with confidence. This will stop unnecessary pondering about the answer. The result will be a decided increase in your speed as well as your knowledge. Knowing why choices are wrong is, of course, crucial to those questions where none or more than one of the choices may be the correct answer.

If you get into the habit of learning why wrong choices are wrong, you will automatically begin to check yourself as you do the questions. If you come across a wrong answer and you do not know why it's wrong, you will at once realize that there is a gap in your knowledge. That choice could appear in a Roman numeral question where you are required to know if it is right or wrong. Those who want to know only the right answer find many questions where more than one choice appears to be correct, even though the question calls for only one correct choice.

When you start reading wrong choices and the reason why the choice is wrong flashes through your mind, you'll know that your study methods are paying off. An added bonus is that wrong answers are repeated. You may find a similar wrong answer on several different questions. Think of the time you will save.

If you answered correctly because you knew the answer, verify that your reasons are the same as those given in the sample answer. Do not go on to the next question until you are sure you would answer this one correctly (and for the right reasons) if you saw it again.

Repeat this process for questions 2 through 10. Be sure that you read the sample answer after each question. Use tabs or bookmarks to go back and forth between the pages with the questions and those with the answers. If this is too cumbersome, cut out or make a copy of the answer or question pages. I do not recommend cutting pages unless you are sure you will not lose the loose pages.

Also, cover the answers until you need them so you will not accidentally learn the answer to the next question. This will, of course, be easier if you are using a computer program and can bounce back and forth with the click of a mouse. Keep studying ten questions, one at a time, in each subject until you consistently score 50% in that subject. You can then go on to the next step in that subject and *only* in that subject. If, at any point in your studies, you find yourself doing poorly on practice tests in any subject, go back to the ten-question, one-at-a-time exercise for that subject.

## STUDY TIP

We have all had the experience of dozing off while studying. Even more often than falling asleep, we have read several pages and afterward had no idea what we read. This happens most often when we are tired or the subject matter is not especially dramatic.

When you find yourself in this situation, study some sample questions. You cannot let your mind wander. As soon as you lose your concentration, you'll know it. If you are too tired to do a few questions, I guarantee you're too tired to study any other way. Studying from Multistate questions and answers will work when studying from outlines will not. For those of you who must study late at night after a hard day's work, it may be the only way you can concentrate enough to truly benefit from your efforts.

# TWENTY QUESTIONS

Once you are consistently at 50% or more correct in a subject, increase the number of questions to 20 at a time. The 50% level sounds easy. It's not. Remember that there are four choices. When you get to 50%, it usually means that you know quite a bit of law. You have not really learned the test yet.

In this exercise, if you believe you know the correct answer to a question, go on to the next question. Go directly to the sample answers only after questions to which you do not know the answer ("not sure" means "do not know"). After finishing all 20 questions, go back and see how many of the answers that you *knew* were actually correct. If you got some wrong (and you will) *reread each question again and then the sample answer.*

As you have probably figured out by now, I believe that you only benefit from the sample answer if you clearly remember the question. To do 10 or 20 questions and then read 10 or 20 answers is almost worthless. Each question must be fresh in your mind when you read the answer. The reason for this is to put you "in contact" with the bar examiners.

# THE DIALOGUE

The Multistate exam is a continuing dialogue between you and the examiners. Imagine for a moment that you are sitting in a room with the bar examiners discussing the test. You tell them your reasons why you like the right answers and do not like the wrong answers. Then they tell you their reasons. After many hours of these discussions, your reasons and their reasons become more alike. You *know* what they're going to say before they say it. You understand how they think. You are ready to take the test. You will never get this understanding from an outline or from practicing sample questions.

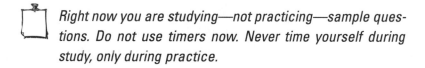 *Right now you are studying—not practicing—sample questions. Do not use timers now. Never time yourself during study, only during practice.*

This is the only part of the bar exam where you can gain this understanding. This is the only part of the exam where they actually give you the answer. They do not decide if they like your answer. You decide if you like their answer. The ability to get an outstanding grade is totally within your control. There is no variation from reader to reader, as may exist on essay questions. There is no one who doesn't like your style, your spelling, can't read your handwriting, is in a rotten mood, has a headache, etc.

## ENGLISH AS A SECOND LANGUAGE

For those of you whose first language is not English, the process of making a scratch mark on a paper compared to expressing your thoughts in just the right words can be an enormous advantage. In your language study, you learned the difference between your active and passive vocabulary. This is the only part of the exam that tests only your passive vocabulary.

## VARIATIONS

Another important reason to become so familiar with the sample questions is how close they are to the ones you are going to get. How many ways can you ask a question on a specific subject? You will not get repeat questions from previous exams, but, if you study properly, the questions will seem familiar.

## ANALYSIS

Next, start analyzing the wrong choices. This should begin to occur to you automatically from your prior work. As stated above, the sample answers in many instances will point out the same reasons over and over again why certain choices are wrong. You will now develop the ability to see wrong answers by learning the *wrong answer techniques* used by the bar examiners. This takes you to one correct answer as opposed to a toss up between two answers that, to the untrained eye, appear equally correct. After you get good at it, the subtle differences are almost glaring differences.

The common thread that you will learn to recognize is that the wrong answer:

- is an incorrect statement of law (always wrong);
- misstates the facts (wrong for this question); or,
- is correct law but either not complete or does not directly answer the question.

Do not think you'll be able to recognize these techniques without doing at least several hundred questions as described above. Surveys by bar review courses estimate that people preparing for the Multistate average about 1,000 practice questions. Some do 3,000 to 4,000. I believe that you can do half the average and still do well if you do them one at a time. Remember to have confidence in the examiners. Their reasoning is consistent. The wrong answer, in some way, doesn't answer the question asked. The easy ones are misstatements of law. The tougher ones are abstractly correct but, again, do not exactly answer the question being asked.

## PRACTICE

At this point, let me interject a word about *practice*. After a few weeks of *study*, you will probably want to start checking your progress. Do 20 or more questions in a row. Do not bother to read the answers. Just use them to get your score. However, if you do want to read an answer, always reread the question first. I recommend at least 20 questions at a time because fewer will not give you an accurate score. This is also the proper format for timing yourself.

To keep study and practice separate, I recommend purchasing the practice book from the National Conference of Bar Examiners. The book will contain sample bar questions and answers without explanations. You will not be able to find out why choices are right or wrong.

The questions may be on the same subject or mixed, depending on whether you use a question book by subject or a sample bar exam. Be sure to use sample bar exams when exam time is getting close as these are the closest tests to the real thing and you should get used to switching subjects from question to question.

There are several exercises to do once you believe that you are getting some knowledge of the test as well as the law.

## EXERCISE

Try answering questions without reading the facts. It's not as hard as you may think. The purpose is to identify wrong choices that do not depend on the facts.

---

# EXAMPLE:

The call of the question asks if a contract was formed.

(a) Yes, because the buyer relied on the seller's oral promise.
(b) Yes, because the goods were specially made.
(c) No, because the contract violated the Statute of Frauds.
(d) No, because the seller shipped nonconforming goods.

Choices (a), (b) and (c) are all possibly correct depending on the facts. In a Roman numeral type question, both (a) and (b) could be correct. We can, however, eliminate (d).

---

Shipment of nonconforming goods is both an acceptance and a breach. You can't have a breach if you do not have a contract. You know that this choice is wrong.

The real benefit to this exercise is that you have to know the law to eliminate the wrong choices. Since you do not have the facts to lead you to the right choice, you need a greater knowledge of the law. Once you go back and read the facts and the sample answer, you'll see that with a complete understanding of that area of the law you could have eliminated more wrong choices. When you get close to the time for the exam, you should pick the correct choice with some frequency.

## EXERCISE

Read the facts and the call and anticipate the correct choice. This is a little easier because you simply have to know the answer. There are two benefits to this exercise. First is the obvious one of testing your knowledge. Second is seeing how another choice might look correct if you did not really know the answer and were depending on the choices to help you. Most people who have trouble with the Multistate say that there are frequently two choices that appear to be correct.

Here is another exercise to eliminate the
"two apparently correct choices" problem.

## EXERCISE

Read the facts and call of the question. Identify the question you are being asked. Write it down to emphasize its importance. Now go to choice (a). Ask yourself if this choice correctly answers the question. Make a mark to indicate your decision (either T or F, or + or -). Now go to choice (b). Refer again to the question being asked. Does choice (b) correctly answer it? Repeat the process for choices (c) and (d). Evaluate each choice independently and do not compare them to each other. Here is an example to illustrate the purpose of this exercise. This is an Evidence question.

---

## EXAMPLE:

Witness is offering testimony as to what witness heard X say as X was viewing the accident in question. X is now deceased. The call asks if the testimony should be admitted.

    (a) Yes, as a present sense impression.

    (b) Yes, because declarant X is unavailable.

    (c) No, because it is Hearsay, not within any recognized exception.

    (d) No, because the statement of a deceased person can never be admitted as evidence (obviously wrong).

---

## ANALYSIS

Let's examine the choices. If I told you that the correct choice is either (a) or (b), could you tell me which one is correct and which is not? Could you tell me why? If we try it using our exercise format, it becomes very easy.

First we read the facts. This is obviously Hearsay. If you are asked about admissibility, you are asked if any of the choices contain an exception to the Hearsay Rule, which fits the facts. You have now identified what the question is asking. You write this down.

Choice (**a**) gives us Present Sense Impression, a recognized exception to the rule. We compare it to the facts and make a decision.

Choice (**b**) makes us ask ourselves the question, again. Does this choice give us an exception to the Hearsay Rule? Our decision is easy. Unavailability is not a recognized exception to the Hearsay Rule. It is a requirement of some exceptions but is not by itself an exception. We can't admit Hearsay testimony by simply showing that the declarant is unavailable.

Why would anyone miss such an easy question? Those of you who missed it probably did so for one of two reasons. The first possibility is that choice (b) fit the facts. X was dead (unavailable). Some of you equated this with the choice being correct. While it is true that a choice must be supported by the facts, you can't stop there. The choice must answer the question.

The second possibility is that you related choice (b) to choice (a). You asked yourself if unavailability was necessary for the Present Sense Impression exception. It's not, but if you did not know that, you felt that this was a more specific choice and, therefore, the better answer.

This is another typical example of a Multistate question. You have two chances to answer the question correctly. First, if you knew the law *completely* regarding Hearsay exceptions, you would know that choice (b) is incorrect law. Second, if you knew the test, you would know that choice (b) does not answer the question being asked. Even if unavailability were required, it would only strengthen choice (a), *not* make choice (b) correct.

The examiners are asking if you know the law and, if not, do you know the test. An area as frequently tested as Hearsay exceptions should be learned completely. But suppose you forgot this exception. Your knowledge of the test will allow you to pick the correct choice while those who studied only the law and forgot can just guess.

This exercise teaches you to never relate choices to each other. Always relate each choice back to the question you have been asked. The choice you pick eliminates all the others. You are left with the facts, the call, and the choice you picked. If the choice you picked depends on another choice, it is wrong. It must independently be correct.

Repetition of this exercise will greatly reduce confusion as to which choice *better* answers the question. Only one choice answers the question. Even on those questions that ask which choice *best* answers the question, only one choice will truly answer the question. (I have yet to find two correct choices to a question requiring one answer.)

If the question instructs you that none or more than one choice may be correct, you still use this process. The difference, of course, is that no choice or more than one choice will *independently* answer the question.

The most important benefit that you will get from any of these exercises is to familiarize you with the test. The more you "play" with the sample questions, the easier they'll become. You are truly, as the saying goes, trying to learn them backwards and forwards, inside and out. Once you realize how well you are learning the law as well as the test, you'll begin to look forward to putting down your outline and *studying* some sample questions.

# FIRST IMPRESSIONS

The next exercise concerns speed. There is no need to do this exercise unless you are worried about finishing on time or you frequently go back and change answers after you finish a practice test.

## EXERCISE

Do 25 questions. Read the question, the call, and the choices carefully. Mark the first impression you get of the correct answer. Do not rush, but do not reread the question or take time pondering. Before looking at the answers, do the same 25 questions. Take your time. Reread the question if you feel it is helpful. Reread your choices as many times as you want. Mark the choices that differ from the first time you did the questions.

Most of you will find little difference in the number of correct answers. Many of you will do better with first impressions.

This exercise will do two things for you. It will enable you to increase your speed with confidence, because you know that pondering over the choices will not get you more correct answers. It will only slow you down.

It will also alert you to a problem if you do much better by taking more time. Now you will have to pay more attention to the clock and perhaps use first impression choices for those questions that seem especially difficult (usually your weakest areas), and then come back to them later if you have time. This way if you get some wrong on those you hurried, at least those are the ones you probably would get wrong anyway. You'll know from your practice tests which areas are most difficult and time consuming for you.

# SKIPPING QUESTIONS

Everyone should be prepared to skip a few questions. No matter how much you know, there will be a few questions that seem especially difficult for you. Even if you do not skip any, you should be prepared. The importance of being prepared to skip some questions is that you are not going to worry about them.

Here's what happens if you are not prepared: first, you spend too much time on the question. You think that you have to answer every one. When you realize that you have spent too much time on it, you put down an answer (probably wrong) and go to the next question.

The next thing that happens is that you keep thinking of that question after you move on. You lose your ability to concentrate on the next question or two. You also hurry through the next several questions because you know that you lost some valuable time.

When you are prepared, here's what happens: you read the question. You quickly realize that it's going to be more difficult for you than most of the other questions. You mark something down and move on to the next question.

You completely forget about that tough question and concentrate on the current one. You knew that there were going to be some questions that you would skip. Remember that you can miss 40-50 questions and do well. You saved a little time by skipping the question so you do not feel rushed as you proceed.

## Avoid Wasting Time

There are two ways to skip questions. The first is to attempt to answer the question and realize that you simply have little or no idea as to the correct choice. This is not really skipping a question. It is deliberately avoiding wasting time on a question that you will probably get wrong.

Pondering is always to be avoided. If you are unable to come up with an answer after about ten seconds of thought, after you have read every part of the question, you are most likely not going to come up with one that you can put down with confidence. Move on.

## Truly Skip

The second way is to truly skip the question. You look at the question. It is especially long and covers an area of the law that you find exceptionally difficult. You immediately go to the next question. The time spent on the skipped question was no more than 15-30 seconds. This is what you must do if you consistently fail to finish your practice tests on time. Do not wait, as most bar reviewers advise, until you have five minutes left and ten questions left. You decide which questions to skip. Do not let the clock decide for you.

Those last ten questions may be ones that you have an excellent chance to answer correctly.

Being prepared means being in control. Even skipping questions requires preparation.

## EXERCISE

Do 20 questions with a timer. Try to determine two or three of the most difficult ones (spending only 15-30 seconds on each) and skip them. See how it affects your time and your score. Your goal is to finish each three-hour test at least five to ten minutes early. You have 36 minutes for each set of 20 questions or 180 minutes for 100 questions. If you can cut that to between 32 and 33 minutes per 20 questions, you are in good shape. After you get good at this, try to cut the number of questions skipped.

When you have finished, try to answer the questions that you skipped. If you find them difficult, you know that you are skipping the right ones.

## SHORTEN THE TEST

There is an extreme measure you can use for skipping questions. If you have tried everything and you still can't finish on time, you might want to shorten the test. This is only to be used as a last resort.

Instead of having a 200 question test, make it a 190, 180, or even a 170 question test. Every time you come to a question on a certain subject, skip it. Of course, make it your worst subject. Let's use the most extreme example. Every time you come to a Real Property question, skip it. If you finish with time to spare (you skipped 30 questions), go back and finish as many as you can.

Before you go to this extreme, try every other method and exercise. This is for those who consistently have 40 to 50 questions left unanswered when time expires on your practice tests. If you skip 30 of the toughest questions for you, you should finish on time.

## MARK AN ANSWER

Skipping a question does not mean skipping an answer. You always mark an answer on your answer sheet. There have been instances when a person has failed to do this and ended up with the questions not corresponding to the answers. Imagine realizing that you are marking answer 99 and you are on question 100. Even if you do not skip questions, it's a good idea to check every few questions to make sure that your questions and answers have the same number.

Each time that you skip a question, mark an answer on your answer sheet and put a mark beside the skipped question in your question book. If you finish early, go back and review the questions that you skipped. There should be, at most, five or six. (If you skipped ten or twenty, you weren't ready to take the test.)

Of the five or six that you marked, try to find the easiest ones. Do those first. (Easiest means that you have some idea what they're asking and some knowledge of that area of the law.) Short questions are preferred.

 *I recommend that you do not go back to questions that you did not skip. In other words, the ones that you weren't quite sure of the correct answer. Leave these alone. Your answer is probably correct. When you redo the ones that you did skip, anything that you get right is a bonus. No pressure.*

I cannot repeat too often that all questions are equal in scoring. Whether it's on the test or in planning your study time, emphasize the areas in which you have the best chance to get correct answers.

## EXERCISE

I have found that for most people, the Multistate questions require a particular state of mind. In other words, a little warm up may be necessary.

Check your practice tests, especially the ones with 50 or more questions. If your bar review doesn't give any long practice tests, take several on your own. Within a week or two of the bar exam, check your score on the first 25 questions against the rest of the test. If you find that the score on the first part of your test is appreciably lower than the rest, you need a warm-up.

What you need to do are some practice questions just before entering the exam room. Copy ten questions (you may find that five is a sufficient number). You should have these on paper that you can throw away before entering the exam room. Do these questions just before the exam instead of talking with friends, as is the usual routine. Know the answers to these questions. You are not trying to learn anything. You are just getting your mind adjusted to the test. You also get a little confidence boost by answering five or ten questions correctly before you even begin the test.

It is important that you do this. You will not only get a few extra correct answers, you will save time and avoid a possible loss of confidence from struggling through the first few questions. Again, be sure that you know the answers to the practice questions. The last thing that you want is to know that you got something wrong before the test even started.

Confidence plays a key role in your success on the exam. This is why you study the test in so many different ways.

## MASTERY MARKERS

☐ I *study* each question by reading the question and, after making my choice, I study the complete answer including explanations of the incorrect choices. I never go on to the next question until I fully understand the current one.

☐ My knowledge and confidence guide me as to when to move on to the next exercise.

☐ I do the skipping questions exercise regardless of whether or not I have a problem finishing on time. This allows me to be prepared should the problem arise on the exam.

☐ I will remember to do my warm-up questions just before practice exams and entering the examination room for the bar exam. This will save me the time to get acclimated to the test.

# ADDITIONAL NOTES:

# SPECIAL EXERCISES 6

You have tried all the above and still cannot get enough right answers. It is time for more drastic measures. This has nothing to do with finishing on time.

## THE ESSAY APPROACH

This is very time consuming, but effective when all else fails. Start writing out the answers using the IRAC (Issues, Rules, Analysis, Conclusion) method. Treat the question as though it were an essay question. Identify the issue or issues. State the rules of law. Analyze the application of the law to the facts. Reach a conclusion. After doing several of these, you can do them in your head. It is time consuming to write out the IRAC method, but you can think of it in seconds once you get used to it.

In essay questions, your issues and analysis count for almost all the credit and you spend most of your time on them. The major difference you will find in the Multistate question is that the conclusion is all-important, since there is a definite answer to the question.

You don't worry about a detailed analysis. You just do enough to get you to the conclusion. This is why you can do them so quickly.

---

# EXAMPLE:

Seller enters into a written contract to sell goods to Buyer. Buyer is to purchase 100 units per month at a price of $50 per unit for a period of one year. The contract states that Buyer's payments are to be made directly to C, a creditor of Seller. Buyer receives the goods for the first month and sends the $5000 payment to Seller. Seller accepts the payment. C then becomes aware of the contract and sues Buyer. The call of the question then asks if one, both or neither of the following is correct.

I.   C is an incidental beneficiary of the contract and, as such, does not have a sufficient interest to sue Buyer. C will lose.

II.  C is an intended creditor beneficiary and, as such, has a right to the payment. C will win.

Your choices are:
   (a) I only
   (b) Both I and II
   (c) II only
   (d) Neither I nor II

---

This is a difficult question because by now you are concentrating on the choices rather than the facts. Number I is obviously wrong and you dismiss it. Number II appears to be just as obviously right.

Now let's look at this as an essay question. The facts are the same, but now you are asked to write whether C would win or lose, and why.

What is the major issue? Did Buyer breach the contract with respect to C? The contract is between Seller and Buyer, but mentions C. C is an intended creditor third party beneficiary who obviously has rights in this contract. What's the next issue? When do C's rights vest?

If you were writing this as an essay question, you would first show the reader that you knew something about third party beneficiary contracts. You would start by saying that a third party beneficiary contract is one formed by two parties for the benefit of a third party. You might give a brief example, say a life insurance policy between the insurer and the insured for the benefit of the beneficiary.

You would then explain that the third party must be an intended beneficiary of the contract and not just happen to benefit incidentally.

Next, you would distinguish between an intended donee or creditor beneficiary. The donee may sue only the promissor on the contract. The creditor may sue both the promissor on the contract and the promissee on the underlying debt.

Finally, you would write that the rights of the third party do not vest until that party has assented to the contract.

Let's look at our question. First, did Buyer breach the contract? Buyer paid the money directly to Seller (a breach of the contract), but Seller accepted the payment. When the conduct of both parties to a contract is different from their express agreement, there is either a modification or waiver. Therefore, once Seller accepted Buyer's payment, Buyer was no longer in breach with respect to Seller.

Next, when do C's rights vest? There may be some discussion as to what constitutes assent to the contract, but certainly knowing of it is a minimum requirement. Therefore, with respect to this payment, Buyer and Seller modified the contract before C's rights had vested. C loses. Both I and II are wrong. The correct choice is (d).

Once you realize that many of the Multistate questions could be asked as essays, you may start picking up the issues that are raised. The question we just did should teach you two things. The first is in your reading of the question.

If you missed the answer because you did not catch the time sequence as to C's becoming aware of the contract, you learned that time sequences, especially in contract questions, are of major importance. You may need to do your exercise (given below) to remember facts.

The second thing you should have learned is some law. When one party to a contract does something different from the agreement without a legal excuse, think breach. When both parties to a contract do something different, think modification or waiver. When there is a third party beneficiary, you must decide if the third party has rights (incidental or intended beneficiary), against whom the third party has rights (donee or creditor beneficiary) and when the third party beneficiary has rights (vesting). Answering this as an essay question necessitated your learning this.

Do you see how much you can learn from one sample question if you really study it? In addition, you are beginning to train your mind to triggered responses. You will eventually zero in on the important points of each question. The "if," the "who," and the "when" will automatically flash through your mind. You cannot get all of this from an outline.

This exercise also works well when two choices appear correct in many questions. If this seems to be your problem, this exercise may pinpoint your weakness. The usual weakness is not knowing the law well enough. If you do not know all the rules or cannot relate them to the facts, the following exercise should help.

# THE TEACHING APPROACH

## EXERCISE

The best way to learn the law is to teach the law. Find a study partner and explain to him or her the law for the areas of each subject most frequently covered on the test. Then answer his or her questions. If it's not possible to find a suitable partner, increase the number of "one-at-a-time" study questions in that area of the law.

Another problem is not remembering the facts. You'll probably be aware of this because you'll keep referring back to the fact portion of the question and have trouble finishing on time.

A good way to test for this is to take a fairly involved and difficult question and take all the time you need to answer it. If this would be an easy question if you had ten minutes to answer it, you know your problem.

## EXERCISE

Start with a short question on one of your better subjects. Read the facts in the question once. Write down the important facts. Read the facts again. Add to your fact list. Read the facts again. Are some facts still missing from your list? If so, you need to keep doing this exercise. When you can recall easy fact patterns, move on to more difficult ones. If you can do even four or five per week, you should see significant improvement.

A memory method that may help is to picture yourself reading the facts to a class. You have been in school most of your life. You should be able to form a mental image of yourself reading in front of a class. I'm not a memory expert but I am passing on advice from memory experts. It's worth a try.

---

# MASTERY MARKERS

❏ When the exercises in Chapter 5 are not doing enough, I will answer the multiple-choice questions as essay questions.

❏ I can try to teach the law that I am trying to learn.

❏ If remembering facts is a problem, I can do the writing exercise and read to an imaginary class.

# ADDITIONAL NOTES:

# IMPROVING YOURSELF 7

If you are reading this book a year or two before you plan to take the bar exam, or you have taken the exam unsuccessfully more than once, you may want to look into some self improvement courses.

I am suggesting this to those of you who know that you have a specific problem like reading too slowly or not remembering what you read. Most of you, of course, would not have made it this far if you had these problems. However, law school exams don't have the extreme time constraints of the bar exam. Rereading questions in law school (usually essay questions) isn't a problem. Slow reading or rereading on the Multistate will mean that you won't finish.

If the suggestions in this chapter don't help, be sure you practice skipping questions, as discussed in Chapter 5.

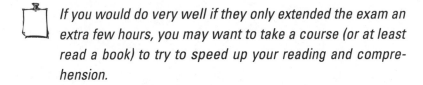 *If you would do very well if they only extended the exam an extra few hours, you may want to take a course (or at least read a book) to try to speed up your reading and comprehension.*

# SPEED READING

I suggest that you begin with a speed reading course or book. This will be broken down into two sections. The first will consist of exercises to increase your reading speed. The second will be concerned with your retention. In the terminology of speed reading, comprehension means remembering, not understanding. Understanding will only come from your knowledge of the law and the test. You should know within a few weeks if it is helping.

If you still have the problem, especially with retention, you might want to try either a memory or self-hypnosis course.

All of these courses are on tape and can be studied at home.

I am suggesting this as an extreme measure. I believe that almost everyone can do well on the exam by being truly prepared, as I have described in the prior chapters. This is only if all else, including this book, fails to give you the necessary improvement.

## MASTERY MARKERS

☐ The suggestions in this chapter are to be used as an extreme measure if all other exercises do not produce my desired results.

☐ A course in speed reading should improve both my reading speed and my comprehension (remembering the facts of the question).

# ADDITIONAL NOTES:

# THE MULTISTATE SUBJECTS 8

Since this book is an approach to learning the test, I will not try to second-guess the examiners. Your bar review will give you up-to-date information on what to expect on your particular exam. The examples I will use are not meant to be all you must know on each subject, or even each question.

This chapter will contain some basic approaches to studying and to answering exam questions that should be used to give you an advantage, both on the Multistate and Essay portions.

Different subjects should be studied in different ways. Some are easier than others. Let's start with one of the easier ones.

## TORTS

As you are aware from your law school studies, Torts does not have a common thread. Trespass to land, Defamation, Interference with a Contractual Relationship and Negligence have only one thing in common: the way you study them. Most students find Torts an easy subject because most of the concepts are simple and the cases are interesting, compared to, say, Civil Procedure or Real Property. To make Torts even easier, always approach it the same way. We'll use Negligence as an example.

Negligence is a heavily tested theory on the Multistate and you must learn it completely. You can get all or almost all of the negligence questions right. Here is how you do it.

Always start with the Plaintiff. As you know, the Plaintiff must prove every element of any Tort or else the Defendant wins. For Negligence, the Plaintiff must prove that the Defendant owed a duty to the Plaintiff, breached the duty (failed to use reasonable care), and the breach caused (actually and proximately) the Plaintiff's damages.

That's it. That's how you study. Every time you identify the question as concerning Negligence, you ask, in order, if each of the four elements (duty, breach of duty, causation and damages) is present. At first you do this consciously, so that later you will do it automatically.

The most common error made is to go immediately to what you believe to be the issue upon which the conclusion will be based. This is an error for two reasons. One, it will take you longer to learn the elements of each tort if you do not review them each time you analyze a particular question. Second, on your essay questions, you will not tell the reader that you know all the elements. Since all elements must be present for the plaintiff to win, leaving out the ones that are obviously not disputed will cost you points. You must show that the plaintiff proved each one, or, at least, mention that some elements are given (not in dispute).

# LEARNING THE ELEMENTS

If you were asked to teach a youngster the numbers from 1 to 10, would you say they are 6,3,4,8,1,9,7,2,5,10? Do not make it tough on yourself. Learn all the elements to each tort in order and review them in your mind, in the same order, every time you identify a particular tort.

So much for the plaintiff. Once you're certain that all elements are established and there is a Prima Facia case, you move to the defenses. Using the Negligence example, you will most likely have Contributory Negligence on the Multistate, and either Contributory or Comparative Negligence on an essay question. Assumption of Risk is usually reserved for Strict Liability questions.

What is Contributory Negligence? It is simply Negligence by the plaintiff. There is no requirement for Contributory Negligence that the plaintiff cause injury to the defendant, only that the Plaintiff's negligence contributed to Plaintiff's injury or property damage. Comparative Negligence has the same negligent conduct requirement as Contributory Negligence. The difference is that you only have to establish that there was Contributory Negligence, no matter how slight. Comparative Negligence, as the name implies, is concerned with the degree of Negligence by the Plaintiff (as a percentage) compared to the degree of Negligence by the Defendant. If you're dealing with Contributory Negligence, do not forget the Doctrine of Last Clear Chance. But you knew that.

So what's your task? Learn the elements of each tort. Study the sample questions to apply your knowledge. If you have a halfway decent memory, Torts should take only a couple of days to learn.

*Remember, you should be refreshing your memory. If you're a first year law student, do not expect to learn Torts in a day or two. There has to be some memory to refresh.*

The exercise that works especially well for Torts is to attempt to answer the question by reading only the call and the choices. Torts questions are filled with wrong law choices and choices that do not answer the call (question).

# CRIMINAL LAW

Do the same thing you did with Torts. Learn the elements of each Common Law crime. If all of the elements are not established, stop. The state loses. Once the state establishes every element of the crime, then look for defenses. If there are no valid defenses, the defendant is guilty. If there are, the defendant is not guilty.

There is another common type of Criminal Law question. This type contains a statute. A statute is simply a fact. It is given and you believe it. Even if it contradicts the law as you know it, believe it. The problem with a statute is that it must be applied exactly as given. If you do not remember facts well, you may have to reread it. This takes time. Use questions containing statutes when you are doing an exercise to help you remember the facts of a question.

# MENTAL STATE

An area frequently tested is the mental state of the defendant. In order to answer correctly, you must know the four mental states and what is required to prove each one. The mental states are Specific Intent, Malice, General Intent and Strict Liability (no intent). How do you know which crimes require which mental state? You memorize them.

## Specific Intent Crimes

The reason it is so important to know the specific intent crimes is that, on the bar exam, a defense that seems ridiculous may be valid.

---

## EXAMPLE:

Defendant gets into victim's Volkswagen. The keys are in the ignition and defendant drives away. The charge is larceny. The defense is that defendant thought the car was his Cadillac (mistake of fact). Since this is a specific intent crime, the defense (any mistake), if believed, is valid. If this were a malice or general intent crime, a "reasonable" belief (mistake) would be required as a defense.

---

The first three specific intent crimes to remember are the *inchoate* (incomplete) crimes. These are offers, plans and trying to commit a crime.

*Solicitation* – Asking someone to commit a crime. An example would be offering a bribe to a public official. If the bribe is refused, the crime (solicitation) has been committed. An important thing to remember is that if the bribe is accepted and the charge is bribery, the crime of solicitation merges into the greater crime and cannot also be charged.

*Conspiracy* – Two or more people plan to commit a crime. Things to remember for the bar exam:
1. Make sure there is a crime involved. For example, Joe and Pete plan to break into Joe's house when his wife is away and "steal" the silverware to pawn for drinking money. For Joe to break into his own house and take his own silverware is not a crime.
2. Conspiracy does not merge. Joe and Pete plan to rob the bank and then rob the bank. They can be charged with robbery and conspiracy to commit robbery.
3. Be sure they intend to commit the crime. For example: After a few drinks at the Friday night card came, the men plan the "perfect" bank robbery. The next day the plan is forgotten and nothing further is done. Modernly, this would not be

enough to prove intent. However, at Common Law, only agreement is required. The question will either give a statute or ask for the Common Law answer.

---

## EXAMPLE:

The day after the plan, the men go to the bank, draw the floor plan and time the employees' lunch schedules. A good case for conspiracy under both modern and Common Law.

---

4. Each conspirator is liable for all foreseeable crimes of the other conspirators in furtherance of the conspiracy. On the bar exam the conspirator who stayed in the hideout has the same degree of guilt as the conspirator who shot the bank guard (foreseeable).

*Attempt* – Trying to commit a crime.

1. Be sure there is an effort to commit the crime, not just preparation. "Casing" the bank and buying a gun would not be enough. Going into the bank and hollering "this is a holdup" would be enough. They won't give you some borderline situation on the bar.
2. Impossibility is not a defense. For example, there is no money in the bank.
3. Make sure there is a crime involved. The above example of Joe and Pete breaking into Joe's house would not be a crime even if Joe and Pete believed it was.
4. Attempt merges. If the charge is bank robbery, attempted bank robbery cannot also be charged.

I have gone into some detail of the inchoate crimes because they can be confusing. I'll list the other crimes without much comment.

Remaining specific intent crimes:
- first degree murder (the examiners will give you a statute to follow);
- assault;
- larceny;
- embezzlement;
- false pretenses;
- robbery;
- burglary; and,
- forgery.

## Malice Crimes

These require a reasonable mistake of fact for a defense. They are:
- arson; and,
- second degree (common law) murder.

## General Intent Crimes

These require a reasonable mistake of fact for a defense. They include all other crimes.

## Strict Liability Crimes

There is no intent required, so mistake is irrelevant. These are usually minor offenses (running a red light) but could be more serious (failure to file tax returns). If you get one on the test, there will usually be a statute to follow.

# CRIMINAL PROCEDURE

Criminal Procedure is also tested under the Criminal Law section. This is usually the more difficult area of the subject. One reason for this is that Criminal Procedure requires a much greater focus. The crimes tested in Criminal Law, as discussed above, are similar to the study of Torts. You simply take the most heavily tested crimes, learn their elements, and make a careful comparison of the facts given to the elements necessary to prove the particular crime.

Criminal Procedure is a subject that overlaps into Evidence and Constitutional Law. The range of the possible questions is beyond your ability to cover. It is an area where the bar reviewers earn their money. You must confine your areas of study to those portions of the subject that most frequently appear on the exam. If you are not currently in a bar review course, I suggest you review the Multistate sample questions and work backward to find the areas most frequently tested. Remember that sample questions deal only with material appearing with some regularity on past exams. Criminal Procedure is a subject in which an outline and lists are necessary.

The method for the study of Criminal Procedure is similar to that of Evidence. Much of your effort will come in learning exceptions to rules. For example, you can start with the premise that a valid warrant is necessary for a search in order to have evidence found in the search admitted.

You learn the elements of a valid warrant. You then learn what constitutes a defective warrant. You now need to know when a defective warrant will still allow the evidence to be admitted, and the circumstances that allow a search without a warrant (exceptions).

Studying Criminal Procedure is best done with lists. Make a list, for example, of those instances under which a warrantless search is permitted. Lists can be used for all subjects, but are most helpful when a large number of items must be remembered. There are many exceptions to the necessity for a search warrant, just as there are many exceptions to the Hearsay Rule for Evidence. Review your lists periodically, especially before you study or practice sample questions.

As with the elements of Torts and Common Law crimes, review your lists in the same order each time you study them.

## STUDY TIP

Here's another word on using sample questions to identify areas to study. This method is helpful for any subject. If you cannot find any sample questions on a particular area of a subject, you should spend little or no study time in that area. Outlines, in order to have continuity and be comprehensive, will contain information superfluous to the exam.

# CONTRACTS

The problem with Contracts is the amount of information you need to learn. The study methods, however, are clear. For study purposes, every contract is the same. Every Contract question will fall into only one of three areas on the Multistate. It will be a formation problem, a performance problem, or a remedies problem. Formation and performance are most tested on the Multistate. Remedies will usually be a part of your Contract's essay question (and maybe your Torts' essay question).

# FORMATION

A formation problem occurs when one party says there is a contract and the other party says there isn't. Sometimes the question will ask if a contract exists. A subtler way of asking the same question is to have the suit based on a breach of contract, the defense being that no contract was ever formed. A *crossover* essay question (one that covers more than one subject) could ask, for example, whether there was interference with a contractual relationship (a Tort), the real issue being, "was there a contract?" (Remember Pennzoil v. Texaco?)

Once you've identified that you have a formation problem, you're back to your old method of study. Learn the elements necessary to form a contract. You all know the general elements: offer, acceptance, and consideration or a consideration substitute. You now must learn the elements of an offer, acceptance, and consideration and understand the meaning of each.

A common definition of an offer, for example, is a commitment (intent) that is communicated to an identified offeree and contains definite terms. You now must learn and completely understand: What is meant by commitment? By communicated? Who is an identified offeree? How definite do the terms have to be?

Next, go on to the ability of the offeror to revoke the offer, and when the offer is revoked by Operation of Law. Also, you must learn the differences between Common Law and UCC rules. You have to know whether the offer is to create a bilateral or unilateral contract, whether it needs to be in writing, etc.

This is why most people find Contracts more difficult than Torts. There is simply more to learn. However, if you take it from the beginning, you'll learn it faster than you now believe you can. It is just like Torts, only it'll take a little longer. For example, you learn how an offer may be accepted. Let's say that this is the Plaintiff's position. Then you learn the *defenses*, those things that would negate the attempted acceptance. You then go to consideration and repeat the process. You're learning the elements on both sides, just as you did in Torts and Criminal Law.

The purpose of formation problems is to establish the right of the plaintiff to bring the action. Just as you did in your Negligence example in Torts, you have to establish that this defendant owes a duty to this plaintiff. The difference is that now it is a contractual duty.

## PERFORMANCE AND REMEDIES

Once you establish that a contract exists, you move on to performance. The contract must now be performed, legally excused, or breached.

You first learn the elements that constitute performance, such as when there is substantial performance. You also learn those things that excuse performance, such as impossibility. If you do not find performance, and you do not find that performance is excused, you have a breach. You then go on to remedies.

## DATES

With most contract questions, date sequences are critical. To properly read a contract question, you must organize your dates in order, noting the legal effect of each action on that date. If a set of facts is long or complex or involves several questions, you may want to take the time to jot down some notes as you read. (I am referring to a Multistate question. You will always make notes for an essay question.)

## DEFINITIONS

You have probably heard more than one definition of a contract. The one I like best is that a contract is an enforceable promise. I am partial to this definition because it tells you how to analyze a contract question. You must look at each promise in your question separately. Do not look at the overall agreement. There may be promises that are enforceable, and those that are not, in the same question. There are promises that are enforceable by one side only, such as in options, voidable agreements, and certain Statute of Frauds problems.

## STUDY TIP

The secret to Contracts is no different from Torts or Criminal Law. Try to be as methodical as possible in your study of the subject. Once you get into the habit of reviewing each element of each aspect of your problem, you will learn faster and quickly identify the gaps in your knowledge. If you go straight to the "bottom line," you will not realize what you do not know. Consequently, you will not learn it. Once you get into the habit of doing this, these elements will flash through your mind in fractions of a second. Taking your time to learn them properly now will save you the pondering, which is so deadly on the exam.

# PAYING ATTENTION

You must understand that to really know Contract law takes time and effort. This book does not try to teach you substantive law. The examples I have used are not close to being a complete list of elements to know. You will get a complete list in your bar review course, with emphasis on the areas most tested. Pay very close attention.

If you did well in your law school study of Contracts, you probably need only a moderate amount of study to prepare yourself. If not, your bar review and study methods are crucial to doing well. You may not have time to learn Contracts completely. You will have to rely on your bar reviewer to prioritize your areas of concentration.

# CONSTITUTIONAL LAW

On the subject of Constitutional Law, the examiners are very kind in their questioning. With such a vast area from which to draw questions, they ask the same ones over and over. Not the same exact questions, of course, but they confine your area of study to a small fraction of the subject matter. This is not to say that the questions are easy. It does mean that you can learn areas of the subject in depth that are almost certainly going to be questioned.

---

## EXAMPLE:

If you can distinguish between equal protection and due process, you will most likely get more than one answer correct. The same is true of knowing the definition of strict scrutiny and when this test is used as opposed to the rational basis test or the intermediate scrutiny test.

---

You'll also find that you will study Constitutional Law as part of your work on other subjects. Criminal Procedure will require you to know about search and seizure (fourth amendment). Real Property could have an Eminent Domain question (fifth amendment). A Defamation (Torts) question might involve freedom of speech or the press (first amendment).

I'll repeat it again. How deeply you go into any subject should depend on how much time you can devote to studying. If your time is limited, take the stuff that will most likely be asked and learn it thoroughly. If you miss two or three questions on this subject because you have no idea what they're talking about, that's okay. If you try to study everything and do not have time to really learn the "heart" of the subject, you're in trouble. Constitutional law is one subject on which (unless you have unlimited time to study) you completely rely on the judgement of your bar reviewers.

In Chapter 3 we went through the different formats that are used to ask the questions. Constitutional Law is a likely place to find a paragraph-type question or a paragraph–Roman numeral combination (even tougher).

---

# EXAMPLE:

I. The "End All Wars Now" association challenges a law that requires disclosure of the associations members, alleging a violation of its first amendment rights.

II. Joe Dove files suit with himself and all taxpayers as plaintiffs to limit Federal spending on weapons at the expense of social programs.

III. The "No More Mines" association sues to prevent further mining in the U.S. because it destroys animal habitat and therefore is contrary to public policy.

IV. Rudy Renter files suit against Exclusive City, asking to strike down its zoning laws. His argument it that zoning laws artificially inflate housing prices beyond his means.

Which of the above Plaintiffs will have standing to sue in Federal court?

    (a) I Only

    (b) I And II only

    (c) III Only

    (d) III and IV Only

## ANALYSIS

This question shows the importance of technique. If you didn't read the call of the question first, you would most likely have to reread the paragraphs. The paragraphs on the exam could be three or four times the length of those I used. You can see the time that could be wasted.

Suppose Constitutional Law was your worst subject and you never really understood *standing*. This would be an ideal question to skip. There are certainly easier questions on the exam and you could come back to this one if you had time after finishing. Having said that, let's answer the question.

I. Plaintiff alleges damage to itself and challenges whether the Constitution allows it. You're not concerned whether the plaintiff would win or lose, only the standing to sue. This one would qualify.

II. This suit would require that the spending violated Constitutional limits. The idea that the government should allocate its spending differently is, of itself, not enough to give the plaintiff standing.

III. Although the plaintiff does allege damage to himself, a general attack on zoning laws because they cause higher prices would not be enough. In other words, how much would houses cost if not for the zoning? Who can say? Also, his inability to buy a house would have to outweigh the value of the laws.

The answer is (a) I only.

## EVIDENCE

The rules of Evidence can be complex and difficult. If you do not know the subject well, it will appear to you that all the rules overlap. The problem is that most Evidence questions require a minimum of a two step process. The first step is to identify the applicable rule. This has to be broken down even further. You have to know why the evidence is being introduced, by whom it is being introduced, and when it is being introduced.

# Why It Is Offered

Let's start with why the evidence is being offered. First, evidence must be relevant. You will probably get one question in which the evidence truly has almost nothing to do with the case. The examiners are asking if you are too caught up in the complexities to see the simple. Many will miss this question.

A variation of this question has evidence being offered that is barely relevant but highly prejudicial. The problem is that there will be questions in which the evidence is highly prejudicial but is allowed. It again comes back to the purpose for which it is offered.

# By Whom and When It Is Offered

Once you determine why evidence is offered (for it is truth or to show state of mind; to show good or bad character; for purposes of identity; to impeach, etc.), you can then ask by whom the evidence is being introduced, and when.

---

## Example:

The prosecution introduces evidence to show the bad character of the defendant. The tendency is to say that this should not be admitted. You're right, it shouldn't in the prosecutor's case in chief. However, it can be admitted to rebut evidence of good character first offered by the defendant.

---

The who and when are easy. The question will usually state it. As long as you read carefully, you will not miss that. The real difficulty comes with why the evidence is offered.

## PURPOSE OF EVIDENCE

My suggestion is that you attack the subject from that perspective. Each time you study a question, concentrate on the purpose of the evidence.

---

### EXAMPLE:

D is accused of battery. When asked on direct examination if D hit the victim, D says, "No." The state offers evidence of a prior battery conviction. The correct choice states that prior convictions cannot be offered to show D's propensity to commit this crime.

---

Suppose when asked the same question, D answers, "No. I never hit anyone in my life."

Now you see the choice about propensity to commit the crime. Now it is wrong. The correct choice states that the evidence can be admitted for impeachment purposes. D said he never hit anyone before. The state is saying that he's lying (attacking his credibility). He's already been convicted of hitting someone.

## KNOWING THE RULES

The second part of your ability to answer the question correctly is, of course, to know the rules. Knowing the rule in Evidence usually means knowing the exceptions to the rule. The Hearsay Rule takes about thirty seconds to memorize. The "knowing the rule" comes from learning the exceptions and when they apply. Incidentally, there will probably be at least one question that is correctly answered by the choice that reads "Inadmissible as hearsay, not within any recognized exception." Do not be afraid of that choice if you are unable to find an exception.

Another technique of the examiners is to give you a partially correct choice.

---

## EXAMPLE:

D is disputing the validity of a search warrant issued on the basis of information supplied by an informant. The choice says that the evidence will be admitted *because* the informant was known to be reliable, gave detailed information, and the information turned out to be correct.

---

All this may be true; however, the fact that the information turned out to be correct is not a reason to admit the evidence. If part of a choice is wrong, the choice is wrong. If you see this, take a second look at the other choices for something you may have missed.

# SUBJECTS

Evidence is another subject that requires reliance on your bar reviewer. For those of you who are getting a head start on the test and do not yet have bar review materials, I will give you a few areas that you must know.

## Hearsay

With about 1/3 of the evidence questions asking about Hearsay, you had better know the rule and major exceptions.

## Character Evidence

Know what it is (rules of general reputation testimony, as opposed to testimony of specific conduct), who may introduce it and when, and the difference between Civil and Criminal cases.

## Impeachment

You will probably have at least one question that has the correct choice allowing evidence to impeach which would be inadmissible for any other purpose. The impeachment rule on the test is the least restrictive. You can get almost any relevant evidence admitted if it is proper for impeachment purposes, and some evidence, which may have no relevance except to impeach.

## Best Evidence Rule

The choice that the evidence should be excluded as not being the "best evidence" may be a correct one. More often than not, it is the wrong choice. Of course, you will not know that if you do not know the rule. This is a good example of why, when you study the Multistate questions, you study the reason the wrong answers are wrong.

## Authentication of Documents

Know the definition of a *document*. Know what an expert can testify to, as opposed to a lay person.

## Privileges

Especially know the two types of spousal privilege, limitations on doctor-patient privilege, and what is not covered under attorney-client privilege.

---

### STUDY TIP

Evidence is one of the best subjects to study with lists. As with any list you are learning, review it completely, in order, every time you study it.

---

This is enough to get you started. There are certainly many other rules you will need to know.

 *I know you're tired of reading this, but I'll keep repeating it. If you do not have much time to study, first learn the important areas (those most heavily tested) completely. You can get away with not knowing something they might ask, but if you do not have a handle on things like Negligence, Hearsay, and Common Law Crimes, you're not giving yourself a chance.*

# REAL PROPERTY

Unless this is your first day of law school, you know that this is a difficult subject. How do you prepare?

Real Property is broken down into several subjects that have little relation to each other. Future Interests, Estates in Land, Landlord and Tenant Law, Mortgages, etc., are all covered on the exam under Real Property. However, knowledge of one will not help you with the others. Let's look at some of these areas.

# FUTURE INTERESTS

Some of the bar exam strategists go as far as to suggest that you consider skipping Future Interests altogether. I suggest that you do some Future Interests problems as a study method for organization. Studying the facts of a complicated Rule Against Perpetuities question will help in other subjects with complicated fact patterns. However, do not try to master the rule if it seriously cuts into your time to study other areas.

## STUDY TIP

Let me again stress the theory of studying for the bar exam. It is a pass or fail situation. There is no more credit given for answering the most difficult question on the test than for the easiest. There are no degrees of lawyers. You are one or you're not, based on whether you pass or fail the exam. Barely passing by answering all the easy questions correctly is wonderful.

The point is that many conscientious law students fail the exam because they are so conscientious. The challenge of learning those things that you find most difficult, no matter how much time and effort it takes, is an admirable quality that could cause you to fail the test. Do not become obsessed with what you do not know. The bulk of the questions are in areas anyone who finished law school can learn thoroughly.

Devote the same time to Future Interests you would allocate to any other area that will make up not more than 5% of the exam.

# Rule against Perpetuities

Having said that, I'll give you two tips for the Rule Against Perpetuities. First, know when the rule does not apply, such as in a reversionary interest.

Second, know what happens after the rule is violated. The question will most likely not end with the answer that the rule has been violated. You will have to know who ends up with the property. Again, the main thing is to get what you can out of this subject without hurting your chances on easier subjects.

# Other Topics

The other areas of property law are within the grasp of all of us. Split your study time between your outlines and your practice questions. You may benefit more from your outlines in Real Property than in some of the other subjects. Just make sure you concentrate on the frequently tested areas and do not get sidetracked.

Some of the areas to concentrate on are easements, adverse possession, estates in land, and mortgages. Since the questions must be general enough to cover all those taking the test without favoring the laws of a particular state, Common Law rules should always be what you learn first and thoroughly.

# MASTERY MARKERS

☐ Each subject may require slightly different study methods from me.

☐ I must be consistent in my study habits. Every time I go through elements of a crime, tort, etc., I use the same order.

☐ Repeat all elements even though only one is applicable to the question. If a negligence question, for example, concerns only causation, I still say "duty, breach of duty, causation and damages." Then I address causation.

# ADDITIONAL NOTES:

# ESSAYS 9

Although this is a book about the Multistate exam, I am including a chapter on essays and one on performance. If you are not currently taking a review course, this will give you some idea of what to expect and how to prepare.

## YOUR ESSAY EXAM

Before beginning to discuss writing essays, let's look at the varying tests in different states. The Multistate Essay Examination is currently used in 14 states. It consists of six questions given in a three-hour session. The subjects covered are Agency and Partnership, Commercial Paper, Conflict of Laws, Corporations, Decedents' Estates, Family Law, Federal Civil Procedure, Sales, Secured Transactions, and Trusts and Future Interests.

Contrast this with California, for example, which gives six questions in two three-hour sessions. There's a big difference between writing a half-hour essay and an hour essay. Some of the subjects are also different.

The National Conference of Bar Examiners gives extensive information on all its tests, including sample essay questions. Its web address is **http://www.ncbex.org**.

The first thing you should do is to contact the Bar Association in your state. This can be done on the Internet. Get as much information about the exams you will take (both essay and performance).

# WRITING AN ESSAY

Let's proceed to how to write the exam. The best advice I've ever heard about any test corrected by a reader is that your greatest hope and your greatest fear is that your test is easy to grade.

This sounds like a contradiction. It isn't. What is meant is that you should give the reader every opportunity to give you a good grade. If you turn in a paper that is poorly organized, misses most of the issues, doesn't show proper analysis, and reaches no conclusion, it's very easy to grade. Unfortunately, it won't be the grade you want. Give the reader a paper that's easy to grade in your favor.

# TELL THE READER WHAT YOU KNOW

The most common shortcoming of law students is that they want to go straight to the conclusion and believe that's good enough. Even though your reader is an attorney and knows all about this particular question, you must act as if the reader knows very little. The reader's knowledge is not being graded.

## EXAMPLE:

You answer that Specific Performance is the proper remedy because the property is unique. A better answer is to tell the reader that you know that Specific Performance requires an inadequate remedy at law, a definite and certain contract, can be used based on mutuality, must be feasible, and there are defenses of unclean hands and laches. You don't have to go into prior restraint and freedom of speech unless the question relates to it.

How much you tell the reader depends on the time you have and the importance of the issue (in this case Specific Performance) to the question. If it's the main issue in a question with few issues, you would naturally go into more detail than if the question has many issues and this is a minor one. A great deal depends on your jurisdiction. As I said before, you answer a half-hour essay much differently from a one-hour essay.

If you have only half an hour, state the issue, the rule of law without much detail, show how it applies to your case (again without much detail) and your conclusion. Sometimes the half-hour question will have only one issue and you can go into detail. Your practice essays from your bar review will give you a feel for writing in the required time.

## STUDY TIP

One more thing: in the following paragraphs I say that a conclusion doesn't mean much. In a half-hour essay it may be more important. The question may have a "right" answer because less time is given for analysis. Again, rely on your bar reviewer for the proper emphasis.

# ALWAYS GIVE A CONCLUSION

Don't let your conclusion substitute for analysis. The conclusion, as you should know by now, means nothing. The Supreme Court can split five to four but your conclusion is either right or wrong? Doesn't make much sense, does it?

Conclusions are usually of two types. The first type is the obvious conclusion. If you spotted the issues and did the proper analysis, there is only one conclusion you can reach. Therefore, it's not worth much. The other is the type that can be argued. It's the type made by a lower court, reversed by an appellate court, and then reversed again by the supreme court, five to four. Do you really think anyone cares which way you decided?

# SPOT ISSUES

Spotting issues is the single most important part of the essay answer. You may have had law school professors who appreciated your long, thoughtful answers, and that's as it should be. The bar exam is a different story. Your reader doesn't know you. He or she didn't teach you; there is no personal interest or sense of accomplishment in reading your answer. The reader is reading many papers as quickly as possible. The law review type writing is not appreciated.

What is appreciated is a complete list of the issues, all applicable rules, a concise analysis and a brief conclusion. If this is laid out in such a way that it is easy to follow (easy to grade), even better.

The reason the issues are so important is that they show the reader your ability. As I mentioned earlier, the reader goes over your paper quickly. The depth of your analysis may be overlooked. What can't be overlooked is, "Did you spot the issues?" The reader knows exactly what the issues are, and how many you saw, or didn't see.

## ALLOT READING TIME

The recommended time for reading and organizing your answer for a one-hour essay question is 15 to 20 minutes. You will have to adjust your time for the MEE half-hour questions. The important thing is not to read too fast and miss issues. Some of the answers require very little writing once you know what you're going to write.

## FORMATTED ANSWER

When you have properly organized your answer, you should be able to write your answer from your notes and not have to refer back to the question. One of the worst things you can do is finish your answer and then realize that you missed something. Writing in margins or having arrows pointing to places where additional information should be inserted, unfortunately, makes your paper easy to grade.

Here is a simple format for your essay answers.

- *Use short paragraphs*. Good things go unnoticed when buried in the middle of a long paragraph.

- *Put your issues and anything else you feel is of utmost importance on the left margin (not in the margin).* Essays are read as quickly as possible. An easy way to read quickly is to go primarily down the left side of the page. Many bar reviewers believe that some readers look only at the left side. If your issues are on the left margin, the reader may give you credit without reading much else. This isn't true of every reader, but you don't pick your reader. They all look at the left side.

  Underline or have key words in large letters. Key words anywhere in your answer should somehow stand out. Underlining and larger writing are ways to do this. If you are writing, printing is a good way to call attention to a word or phrase.

- *Don't overdo it.* If you attempt to call attention to almost everything in your paper, you lose the effect and simply give the paper an uneven and sloppy look.

You'll get good advice on format from your bar reviewers. I'm only hitting the absolute musts.

# Caution

I have mentioned several times the wonderful things your bar review will do for you. Let me now criticize a practice of some review courses. The practice I oppose is that of having you memorize a paragraph for each subject, which you write as the opening to your answer. The theory is that you give yourself time to ease into the question and at the same time tell the reader you know something about the subject. This practice is used for one hour essays and doesn't apply to the MEE.

I object to this for two reasons. First, it takes time. I would rather have you reread the question one more time and possibly spot one more issue. Second, I wouldn't want my paper to contain the exact opening as someone else's paper. If I were a reader and happened to get two or three papers with exactly the same opening, I would tend to grade the papers lower rather than take the opening paragraph as a plus. This is only my opinion and you are, of course, free to do otherwise. I have no evidence to show that these paragraphs damage or benefit the grade given.

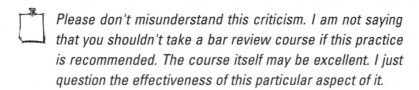 *Please don't misunderstand this criticism. I am not saying that you shouldn't take a bar review course if this practice is recommended. The course itself may be excellent. I just question the effectiveness of this particular aspect of it.*

## SUMMARY ILLUSTRATION

Instead of the usual summary checklist, I'll do a sample question to illustrate the points made in this chapter. Instead of just writing one, I'll point out the style rather than the substance.

On Aug. 1, Yarno, a wholesaler of wool products, received an order by telephone from The Sweater Shop, a retailer of sweaters. The order was for 100 wool ski sweaters, model X, as described in Yarno's catalogue. The wholesale price was $40 each. It was emphasized in the conversation that the sweaters had to be delivered no later than Sept. 1, in order to take advantage of "Ski Week," an annual sales event in the town where The Sweater Shop was located.

On August 10, The sweater shop received an invoice from Yarno acknowledging the order, sweater model, price and delivery date. The invoice was not signed. The invoice also noted that although it would try to comply with the delivery date, it could not guarantee delivery by Sept. 1. On Sept. 2, The sweater Shop purchased 100 similar sweaters at $50 each in order to have them for "Ski Week." On Sept. 3, the sweaters were received from Yarno. They were model Y, not X. A letter received with the sweaters explained that Yarno was out of Model X and was sending Model Y as an accommodation only. The Sweater Shop rejected the shipment and sued Yarno for $1000, the difference between Yarno's $40 price and the $50 price they paid for the similar sweaters.

Discuss the legal issues involved and who would win the suit.

How do you write your answer?

First, you must find the issues. You know that this is a contract question involving the sale of sweaters (goods). That means that UCC law applies, so you write at the left margin:

**Issue**: Does the UCC apply? There is no way the reader cannot know that you spotted this issue. You then go on to explain when Article 2 applies (transactions in goods) and that this covers a sale of sweaters (goods). You might want to give a brief definition of goods, depending on time. You also define a Merchant and state that a Merchant is held to a different standard in certain situations than one who is not a Merchant. In a one-hour question you would also explain that when the UCC conflicts with Common Law, the UCC prevails. When the UCC is silent on any point, Common Law is used. If you are writing a one-half hour answer, you may want to skip this explanation as well as the definition of goods.

After you have decided that the UCC applies, you go to the next issue.

**Issue**: Was there a valid contract between Yarno and The Sweater Shop? Again, the reader can't miss it. You now write:

A valid contract is formed by offer, acceptance, and consideration.

You must now go through a brief description of offer, acceptance, and consideration and how each applies here. You define an offer (serious intent, identified offeree, communication, sufficiently definite terms). For acceptance, you can point out the difference between Common Law acceptance and UCC acceptance depending again on your time (hour or half hour). You may want to simply define acceptance under the UCC. You then go on to consideration.

Of course, do this on the margin as follows:

**Offer**: Definition and application to this case.

**Acceptance**: Definition and application to this case.

**Consideration**: Definition and application to this case.

You will easily find that there are all the necessary elements of formation. You then go to defenses.

**Issue**: Are there defenses to formation?

Define the Statute of Frauds. How much definition you give again depends upon time. You may want to go straight to the UCC requirement of a writing for goods of $500 or more. You now go through the facts (the verbal agreement) and the writing of August 10 (the invoice from Yarno).

**Issue**: Was the unsigned invoice from Yarno of August 10 sufficient to satisfy the requirements of a writing?

List the requirements, apply them to the invoice, discuss what constitutes a signature, decide that it was, and go on to the next issue.

**Issue**: Did Yarno successfully avoid acceptance of the Sept. 1 delivery date?

Go on to discuss whether this was an additional term or a condition of acceptance. If it's an additional term, did it materially alter the contract? Depending on your time, discuss additional terms when one or both parties are not merchants. If it's a condition of acceptance, no contract was formed. You reject that it is a condition of acceptance and go on to the next issue.

**Issue**: Did The Sweater Shop properly cover? You define cover, point out the breach by Yarno, the importance of the delivery date, and decide yes. Next.

**Issue**: Was the Accommodation letter sufficient to avoid acceptance by Yarno? You explain what an accommodation letter is and why this is not one. You explain that an Accommodation letter is used in place of an acceptance, not after acceptance to explain why nonconforming goods are being sent.

You conclude that The Sweater Shop wins. You don't have to conclude this. If you decided somewhere along the way that a contract was not formed, then the Accommodation letter is valid and Yarno wins. The important thing is that you spotted the issues, discussed them by setting out the rules of law and how they apply to this case, and reached a conclusion. You put all your issues where they couldn't be missed. You used short paragraphs.

You will get plenty of practice essay questions in your other books. What I would like you to do is write out the above answer. You have the format and a little law. Use any materials you need to write a complete answer. See how complete an answer you can write in half an hour or an hour. You can estimate by the number of pages you write how much time it would take you writing from memory only. Remember that you must spend sufficient time reading the question to spot all the issues and properly plan your answer.

## ADDITIONAL NOTES:

# PERFORMANCE 10

Some of you will have to answer Performance questions. This part of the test differs from state to state. The Multistate Performance Test is developed by the National Conference of Bar Examiners. There are three possible questions. The reason I say *possible* is that each state may give one, two, or all three on its exam. Each question is supposed to be answered in 90 minutes. The questions must be given on the day before or after the multiple-choice portion of the exam. By contrast, California, for example, makes up its own questions. Each is 180 minutes long.

*Since my interviews with those taking the bar were done in California, I will use that state to illustrate an important point.*

In California, the Performance questions are given on the afternoons of the first and third (final) day of the exam. This means that the last question you do is a Performance question. Bar review surveys and my own interviews of those who failed the bar exam have found that some people are so dejected by the final day that they just want to leave. They put little effort into the Performance question. Later they learn that they were okay to that point and they failed based on the last question. The lesson is obvious. Make up your mind before the first day of the exam that, no matter how you think you're doing, you'll give your best effort to the very end of the test.

# THE QUESTION

What is a Performance question? It is not really a question as we usually think of it. It is a test in itself. It is what is called a *closed universe* test. This means that all the materials you need to complete the task asked of you are given. All of the facts and all of the law necessary for your answer are contained in the question. Theoretically, you could do the task without any prior study of the law. You do your legal research right in the materials given. Here is how it works.

The question starts with instructions from the examiners as to the time allowed and how to write your answer. Next comes the task itself. The usual form will be a letter to you from someone in your law firm. It will inform you that you must do some work on a file. It will give you some background information on the file and then ask you to write something.

There is a wide range of what you will be asked to write. It could be a closing argument to a jury, a letter to a judge, an appeal, a letter to a client, a recommendation to someone in your law firm as to whether to settle or go to trial, a list of questions for a deposition, etc. The Multistate Performance Test description even includes writing a will. The point is that you can't prepare yourself specifically for this task.

Next you will have a portion called the file. The file will contain the specific information of the case. It may contain depositions, letters, documents such as deeds, wills, etc., which give you the facts.

Next will be the library. It will contain cases that will usually reach different conclusions about matters similar to those on which you're working. Most, but not all, questions have libraries.

# THE ANSWER

Where do you start? Identify the purpose of what you are being asked to write. The purpose will be to persuade, to analyze, or to gather information. Once you have determined this, you must follow through on this purpose and not deviate from it. Let's look at some examples.

# PERSUASIVE

You are asked to make a closing argument to a jury or a recommendation of a light sentence for your client to a judge.

When your job is to persuade, that's what you do. What are the pitfalls to avoid?

Never try to distance yourself from your client. You may be asked to defend a client who has done something terribly immoral. Don't try to let the reader know that you personally find this client offensive and in "real life" wouldn't take such a case. You have been asked to perform. Do it. Make the best arguments you can think of, even if they are probably losing ones.

Don't lie. This is the other side of the coin. Remember that this is an exam. Don't get so caught up in persuasion that you misstate or add facts. It's okay to lose as long as you do your best. The question may even contain ethical problems for you.

---

### EXAMPLE:

In a sample question, a client asked for advice regarding a possible divorce. He was thinking of moving to a state having community property laws. His current residence did not. He wanted to know if he would be better off financially to divorce before or after the move. His wife thought their marriage was solid and knew nothing of his plan.

---

This is tricky. You, of course, have to advise him that to move for this purpose would be fraud and the usual laws would not apply. You would also tell him that you could not advise him to perpetrate a fraud. However, you obviously couldn't stop there. You'd still have to contrast the laws of each state and tell him the differences as they would apply to each of the assets he lists in his letter.

The point is that if you simply advised him on the financial aspects and didn't address the ethical problem (both his and yours), you would lose points. You missed an issue.

Next, minimize the law against you. You may, for example, be given a case that goes against your client. You may be required to disclose it. You must *distinguish* this case. This means that you must make it appear to be less important than the cases that favor your client. You do this in any of three ways:

- First, you can argue that the facts are different from the case you are arguing and, consequently, the conclusion reached does not apply. This may be your only argument if the case is one that the court must follow.
- Second, check the jurisdiction. If the court doesn't have to follow the case that you are trying to distinguish (it's from another jurisdiction), you have a second argument.
- Third, and weakest, argue that the decision is wrong. Perhaps you can use a dissenting opinion or a contradicting case.

## ANALYSIS

Give an honest evaluation. If you're advising someone in your firm as to the chances of winning, persuasion has no place in your advice. Give as many pro and con arguments as you can, and then an honest opinion as to the chances of winning. Again watch for possible ethical problems.

## FACT FINDING

If you are asked to write the questions to a deposition, ask yourself what you would want to know from this witness. Don't be afraid to stray a little from the rules of Evidence. You're trying to gain information as well as testimony, even if some of what you learn is inadmissible as evidence.

## TIME AND STUDY

The main problem in studying for the Performance section is time. Since each question takes three hours, you can't do hundreds or even dozens of practice questions.

One way to study is to read practice questions and, as you read, underline or highlight those portions that you would use to write an answer. Formulate the answer in your mind. Then go to the practice answer and see how close you came and if you missed any major points. It's still time consuming, but you should be able to do one in about half an hour.

A more time-consuming but better way to study is to do everything except write the answer. Write down all the relevant issues and outline what you're going to write.

Organizing your answer is critical to a performance question. The National Conference of Bar Examiners suggest for their 90-minute questions that you take 45 minutes to read the question and organize what you are going to write.

If your state requires performance questions, be sure that your bar review offers several sample performance questions complete with answers. You should be required to do at least one question (usually at home) that you can turn in for grading and comments. If not, you may have to take a review specializing in performance (extra cost).

There are, as I mentioned earlier, courses that review only the performance section. The main advantage to these courses is that you will be forced to do many more practice questions than you may do if left to your self-discipline. The more you do, the better you'll get at doing it, especially the organizational part.

# MASTERY MARKERS

☐ I must be certain of the task required before I begin my research and writing. My writing style (persuade, analyze, gather information) depends on knowing the task.

☐ If I am to persuade, I must never try to separate myself from the client, even though in real life I might refuse the case.

☐ Persuasion must stay within the limits of the information given. I must not lie.

☐ If I am to analyze, I must not be concerned if my firm's client wins or loses. Taking sides is for persuasion, not analysis.

☐ If I am to gather facts (deposition), I may stray from the rules of admissible evidence to ask relevant questions.

☐ I distinguish unfavorable cases in the library by first trying to argue that they are not on point. If they are on point, I argue that they are not binding (different jurisdiction). If they are binding, I look for a dissenting opinion to argue that the majority opinion is incorrect.

☐ I must make sure that my bar review offers complete sample questions and will review a practice test.

# ADDITIONAL NOTES:

# THE PRESSURE 11

You've prepared yourself to take the test. Is there anything else that you can do? Yes.

Much has been made of the stress placed upon you by the importance of the exam. How can you minimize it? This advice will certainly not apply to all of you.

## GETTING TO THE EXAM

If you are taking the exam in a city where getting to the morning session will require rising very early and fighting traffic, stay in a hotel near the exam site. Some areas, such as Southern California, offer the exam at hotels as well as other sites. If this applies to your location, get a room at the hotel where the exam is being given. Further, if the hotel offers an executive floor, spend the extra money and book it. You will have a special room for breakfast with no crowds or waiting to be served. You will have a lounge in which to relax in the evening.

Your goal is to be prepared. This means being in control. Depending on your car, lack of traffic congestion or that public transportation will function properly is losing control. If at all possible, start your day within walking distance of the exam site.

# MEALS

The next problem is the lunch break. Bar reviewers usually advise that you know in advance where you are going to eat lunch. They further advise that you have lunch alone and avoid talking to others about the test. This is good advice. I will take it a step further and advise you to have lunch in your room at the hotel. Bring a cooler if necessary and get a sandwich the previous night. If you want warm food, arrange for room service to be delivered at a specified time. I'd rather eat a sandwich than depend on room service.

# WARM-UP

Most bar reviewers also advise that you not study immediately before or between portions of the exam. I concur. The only exception is the warm-up sample questions that you do right before the multiple-choice exam. It doesn't have to be two minutes before. If you have a hotel room, do them just before you go to the test. This should be about fifteen minutes before test time.

# MATERIALS

When you go to take the exam, bring all of your writing instruments (pens, pencils, erasers, highlighters) in a transparent plastic food bag (baggie). The examiners must see everything you bring to the test and it's not a good idea to go fishing through your pockets during the exam.

# GENERAL ADVICE

An obvious bit of advice is to keep all of your vices until after the exam. Just before the exam is not the time to quit smoking. You get the idea. Do whatever is necessary to make things easy for you.

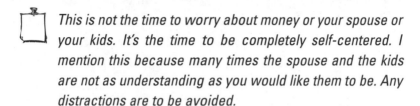

*This is not the time to worry about money or your spouse or your kids. It's the time to be completely self-centered. I mention this because many times the spouse and the kids are not as understanding as you would like them to be. Any distractions are to be avoided.*

By now you should realize that the purpose of this book is to allow you to take the exam feeling that there's not much more you could have done to improve your chances. If you fail your exam, you will be able to concentrate on the specific areas that you need to improve. If your entire experience of studying and taking the test was poorly planned, it will be difficult to pinpoint the problem and correct it.

If your problem is with your support system, I can't be of much help. The only advice I can give you is to keep reminding yourself that the only thing the examiners are interested in is whether you put your little scratch marks in the right boxes. If you do, you're a lawyer. It may upset some of your friends, some of your relatives, and unfortunately for some of you, your overly competitive spouse or companion. However, no one can take it away from you, and insincere congratulations are much preferred to insincere condolences.

## MASTERY MARKERS

I can reduce stress by:

☐ Staying as close to the exam site as possible.

☐ Eating alone or with someone not taking the exam and having meals easily available.

☐ Doing my warm-up exercise.

☐ Doing whatever is possible to make things easier for me, even if I'm being a little selfish.

# ADDITIONAL NOTES:

# PUTTING IT ALL TOGETHER 12

Again (for the hundredth time), the most important things to remember are as follows.

1. *Relevance*—Determine which areas of the law are most heavily tested.

2. *In-depth study*—If your study time is limited, know the heavily tested areas completely, even if it means skipping areas that occasionally are tested.

3. *Confidence*—This comes from doing well on your practice tests. Doing well on your practice tests comes from in-depth studying of relevant material.

4. *Sample questions*—Study sample questions as often as possible and when, for any reason, you don't seem to be benefiting from your outlines. As you find that you benefit more from sample questions than from your outline, you will probably use them as your primary study tools.

5. *Audio*—Audiotapes should be obtained if at all possible. Even if you use them only when your eyes get tired, they will reinforce your memory of the lecture material. Lecture material emphasizes the most heavily tested areas.

6. *Sample answers*—Study by always reading your sample answer before going on to the next question. When you're correcting a practice test, reread each question you missed before reading the answer.

7. *Wrong answers*—Always learn why the wrong answers are wrong, even if you answered the question correctly and for the right reasons.

8. *Pressure*—Don't panic. Familiarizing yourself with the test takes time. Your improvement may not be noticeable until very close to the time for the exam. Remember that every sample question you miss gives you a little more knowledge, both of the law and the test.

9. *Avoidable mistakes*—There's a saying that "Life is tough, and it's a lot tougher when you're stupid." Avoid the dumb mistakes like numbering out of sequence and, above all, give your best effort all the way through the test, no matter how poorly you think you're doing.

10. *Attitude*—The most important change is your approach to sample questions. They should not be viewed as a measure of your knowledge until very close to exam time. They are tools by which you learn both the law and the techniques of the bar examiners. By reading the sample answers to both the right and wrong choices, you will gain both a greater understanding of the subject matter and (you can't get this from an outline) the test. There is no better way to spend your study time.

# A FINAL WORD

The most important point of all is to keep trying. You made it through law school and you'll make it through the bar exam. Every time you do an exercise it brings you a step closer to succeeding. Even if you didn't pass on a previous try, don't be discouraged. This is different. This will work if you make the effort.

Approach the exam realistically. It's not an impossibility. It's a tough test that can be passed without much difficulty after proper preparation. You know what you have to do. Do it and enjoy your law practice.

Finally, let me wish you the "luck" that always seems to follow careful planning and hard work.

# APPENDIX A:

# EXAMPLES

The following are a few typical questions, or parts of questions, asked on the Multistate exam. Pick your choice before reading the explanation. You should by now be able to pick the right choice and explain why it is right and why the wrong choice or choices are wrong.

## CONSTITUTIONAL LAW

There have been many questions over the years that involve, or appear to involve, licenses. An example is a state statute requiring counseling before receiving a marriage license for people under a certain age (but not minors). The question will stress good intentions of the state, such as the parties learning their rights and legal responsibilities. The question will then call for a challenge in Federal court on constitutional grounds.

These questions are sometimes misleading in that the constitutionality of the statute is not involved in the correct choice.

# EXAMPLE:

The facts say that both parties live in the same state and plan to apply for the license shortly. Choice (a) says that the couple can't bring the suit because there is no diversity.

Choice (b) says that they can't bring the suit based on ripeness.

 Answer the question before reading the explanation that follows.

Whenever you find a question with two or more choices that are correct law, you know that the wrong choices do not fit the facts or do not answer the question. Let's look at these two choices.

Choice (a) diversity—Does a lack of diversity automatically disqualify bringing a suit in federal court? No, unless there are no other grounds on which to rely. In this set of facts we can argue that there is a Federal Question. Marriage falls under the right of privacy, which has constitutional protection. The fact that the requirement is based on age might also give us an Equal Protection question.

Choice (b) ripeness—What about ripeness? The couple has not yet applied for or been denied a license for refusing to follow the statute and undergo counseling. Would this automatically disqualify bringing the suit in federal court? Yes, with certain exceptions that don't apply to this case.

If you made a mental review of your list of reasons to file in Federal court, you would have made quick work of this question. After hours of studying sample questions (learning the right answer and all the wrong answers, one at a time), you knew that correct law means correct for this question. You also knew that an incomplete answer might be correct if the facts or choice isolate it. Diversity would be the right choice if the facts or call eliminated the other reasons to sue in Federal Court. Remember that when a choice says because, it makes the reason that follows stand alone. In other words, you're not being asked if the reason is good law. You're being asked if the reason is the only one necessary to answer the question.

Another type of question might go like this (we'll use similar facts):

## EXAMPLE:

State X passes the required counseling law. The statute is challenged. The U.S. Supreme Court rules that the statute does not violate the Constitution. A Federal statute is then passed, which states that no counseling is required for a marriage license. Can state X still require counseling?

    (a)  Yes, because the state statute has been declared constitutional.

    (b)  No

 Answer the question before reading the explanation that follows.

The facts are made deliberately silly for a reason. There are many questions on the exam where the details of the facts don't mean anything. Do we need to know the contents of the statute to eliminate one of the choices?

What is choice (a) telling us? It is telling us that as long as a state statute is not unconstitutional, it is superior to a federal statute that contradicts it. We can easily eliminate this choice as incorrect law.

You can see the difficulty you could create for yourself by worrying about whether marriage is protected as a state right and whether Congress can constitutionally pass such a statute.

They don't require that depth of knowledge on the Multistate. If this question asked you to pick all or none of the correct choices, it would be more difficult. Remember that many of the questions are going to give you more than one reason to eliminate a choice. The quick and easy reason to eliminate the choice will come from knowing the test, not some rule of law that may be obscure or in dispute. If you have to know the law to answer the question, it will almost always be law on a major point stressed by your bar review.

# CONTRACTS

## EXAMPLE:

Buyer writes to seller, ordering 500 units of part X30. Seller writes back acknowledging receipt of the order and agrees to ship the ordered parts within 10 days. Seller subsequently realizes that it has only 400 units of part X30. Seller ships the 400 units of part X30 along with 100 units of part X40, which is interchangeable with part X30. Seller sends a letter with the shipment explaining what has been done and agreeing to take back the X40 parts if Buyer does not want them. Buyer sues for breach. Buyer will:

(a) Win.

(b) Lose, because Seller shipped the nonconforming goods as an accommodation.

 Answer the question before reading the explanation that follows.

If you approach this question properly, it's about as easy as it gets. First, you follow the sequence of events in order and decide on the legal effect of each.

The order by Buyer was obviously an offer. The acknowledgment by Seller and agreement to ship the ordered goods was just as obviously an acceptance. Seller then shipped nonconforming goods, an obvious breach. I told you this was easy.

What about the accommodation letter? You can't get out of your contractual obligations by sending a letter saying that you can't perform. The accommodation letter is only effective when the offer has not yet been accepted. This offer was accepted by promise.

The accommodation letter is used to avoid acceptance and simultaneous breach when the offer is to be accepted by performance (shipping the goods).

If you didn't decide the legal effect of each action of the parties in order, this was an easy question to miss. If you did approach it properly, you got it right even if you didn't know all the U.C.C. rules regarding accommodation. Struggling to remember rules that are not necessary to answer the question is one of the biggest time wasters on the exam.

If you missed this question [the correct answer is (a)], you did not study the essay chapter carefully enough. The accommodation letter issue is the same. This is very important. Many questions will have the same issues as your sample questions with different facts. If you can't identify the same issues when the facts change, you still have work to do.

Here's another example of a straightforward, not too difficult question that could easily be missed:

# EXAMPLE:

Buyer's hobby is collecting hard to find automobiles. Dealer, knowing this, writes to Buyer on May 1: "I have a 1947 Studebaker in mint condition that I will sell to you for $20,000. You have until July 1 to give me your answer." On June 15, having heard nothing from Buyer, dealer sold the car to X. On June 20, Buyer, unaware of the sale to X, wrote to Dealer accepting the offer of May 1. Since Dealer cannot perform, Buyer sues for breach. Buyer will:

I.   Win, because Buyer accepted Dealer's offer and Dealer is unable to perform.

II.  Win, because even though Dealer revoked the offer by the sale to X, the revocation was invalid under the Merchant's Firm Offer Rule of the U.C.C.

(a) I only

(b) II only

(c) Both I and II

(d) Neither I nor II

 Answer the question before reading the explanation that follows.

The Merchant's Firm Offer Rule states that an offer made in writing and signed by a merchant that states it will remain open must remain open for the time specified in the offer, or, if no time is specified, for a reasonable time. The maximum time the merchant is required to keep the offer open is three months, regardless of the time specified in the offer.

This is a rule that you should know for the exam. It is not necessary, however, that you know it to answer this question. Let's take the actions of the parties by date and decide on the legal effect of each.

May 1—Dealer makes a written offer to Buyer to sell Buyer the car.

June 15—Dealer sells the car to X. Dealer is now unable to sell the car to Buyer (to perform). The offer to Buyer has not been affected.

June 20—Buyer accepts Dealer's offer in writing, without knowledge of the sale to X.

Clearly, Buyer should win. We have no Statute of Frauds problem and no revocation. To have a revocation by the sale to X, Dealer would have to notify Buyer of it or Buyer would have to learn of it from a reliable source.

What about the Merchant's Firm Offer Rule? Roman numeral II says that there was a revocation. There wasn't, and so it is wrong, even though all the elements necessary to apply the rule are presented in the facts. (a) is the correct choice.

If we changed the facts and Dealer had notified Buyer of the sale to X before Buyer's acceptance, this would be a question about the Merchant's Firm Offer Rule. As it is, it's a question about attempting to revoke an offer without notifying the offeree. Anyone who took a Contracts course knows that you can't do that.

# CRIMINAL LAW

## EXAMPLE:

Defendant testifies that he has never been convicted of a crime. The prosecution produces records of a prior conviction. Perjury is defined as deliberately giving false testimony. At the Perjury trial, Defendant's explanation is that his lawyer at that time told him that because he was put on probation, he had not been convicted. If the jury believes this, Defendant should be found:

(a) Guilty, because ignorance of the law is not a valid excuse.

(b) Not guilty, because Defendant lacked the required mental state to commit Perjury.

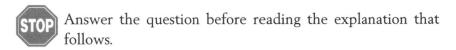 Answer the question before reading the explanation that follows.

This is another simple question, unless you ignore the rules. The only way that you miss this question is if you do not believe Defendant. Don't doubt the examiners. If they tell you that the jury believes that Defendant is from outer space, that's what you believe. Never question something that is given, no matter how unlikely it may sound. "If the jury believes" means that the jury believes.

If the jury believed Defendant, the required mental state was lacking. There was no deliberate false statement. Choice (b) is correct.

Another type of question may go like this:

# EXAMPLE:

Defendant (D) has always admired X'S watch, which is worth several thousand dollars. One night D sees X without his watch. X says he left it at home. D immediately goes to X's house to steal the watch. He breaks in, finds the watch and leaves the house. He is struck by feelings of guilt. He returns to the house, puts back the watch and leaves. He is then arrested. D is guilty of what Common Law crimes?

(a) Burglary and Larceny

(b) Burglary only

(c) Larceny only

(d) Neither Burglary Nor Larceny

 Answer the question before reading the explanation that follows.

If you prepared properly, you know the definitions of Common Law Burglary and Larceny. Do the actions of D fit these definitions? Yes, they do. The correct choice is (a). Why would anyone miss this? The reason to miss this is to get caught up in the practical. Wouldn't this, if it actually happened, be pleaded down to a lesser offense? Most likely.

However, crimes cannot be undone on the bar exam. Once D committed Burglary, the breaking and entering of the dwelling house of another at night with the intent to commit a felony, and Larceny, the taking and carrying away the personal property of another with the intent to permanently deprive the owner of the property, that's it. The Multistate shows no mercy for subsequent remorse. This will also work for Euthanasia killings, which the examiners are not reluctant to put on the exam. Since they will ask about Common Law, present controversies or changes in the law will only confuse you further if you don't concentrate on what they're asking.

# CRIMINAL PROCEDURE

## EXAMPLE:

The police ask the friend of a suspect in a crime to help them locate the suspect. The friend agrees and goes to the precinct to talk to the detectives. During the interview, the friend suddenly says that he cannot stand the guilt and admits committing the crime with the suspect. At trial the friend (now defendant) moves to suppress the confession because the police failed to give the Miranda warning. The court will:

    (a) Suppress the confession because the defendant was in custody and entitled to the warning.

    (b) Suppress the confession because defendant was denied counsel.

    (c) Admit the confession because it was voluntarily made.

    (d) Admit the confession because defendant waived his rights by going to the precinct.

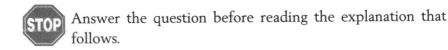 Answer the question before reading the explanation that follows.

**(a)** Being in custody would mean that the defendant was not free to leave. There is nothing in the facts to indicate this.

**(b)** The defendant did not request nor was he denied counsel. The question is whether the defendant knew he had a right to counsel (Miranda warning).

**(c)** Does a voluntary confession require the Miranda warning? The facts tell us that the defendant was not a suspect and the confession was suddenly given. If this were an essay question, it might give you a problem as to when the warning should have been given.

We don't have to worry about that here. If the other three choices are wrong, this is our answer.

(d) Going to the precinct voluntarily would not waive defendant's rights. If he became a suspect at any time before the confession, the detectives should have given the warning before further interrogation.

The answer is clear. All choices except (c) are worded so that they are wrong. If you read and believe every word, we know the answer. It is important that you believe the facts of the question. If you start thinking that the police had an ulterior motive in asking the friend to help them, you're going to miss this question and lots of others. Don't take defendants case. If you were defendant's lawyer, you would make this argument. The given facts do not indicate anything other than the police wanted to have the friend help locate the suspect. That's what you read and that's what you believe.

This example was relatively easy because you didn't have to know much law. You just had to read the question carefully. Usually, the examiners will rely at least as much on your knowledge of the law than your knowledge of the test in this subject. Isolate your areas of study, as emphasized by your bar reviewers and your sample questions. Make lists as was discussed earlier and study them in the same order each time that you review them.

# EVIDENCE

## EXAMPLE:

Pam sued for injuries from a fall at the entrance to a restaurant in an office building. The floor was covered with freshly waxed tile. Pam claims that the amount of wax applied was excessive and created a dangerous condition.

The defendants were Olga, owner of the building, and Rudy, lessee of the restaurant. Olga's defense was that the entrance was part of the property leased to Rudy over which Olga retained no control. Rudy denied negligence and alleged contributory negligence.

1. Rudy offered to testify that in the week immediately preceding Pam's fall at least 1,000 people had used the entrance safely. The trial judge should rule this evidence:

    (a) Admissible, because it tends to prove that Pam did not use reasonable care.

    (b) Admissible, because it tends to prove that Rudy was careful in maintaining the floor.

    (c) Inadmissible, because the testimony is self-serving.

    (d) Inadmissible, because it is not relevant to Pam's fall.

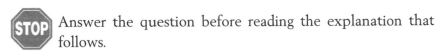 Answer the question before reading the explanation that follows.

(a) This choice is wrong because absence of previous accidents is not admissible to prove that the plaintiff was contributorily negligent (did not use reasonable care) in this case.

(b) This is a variation of choice (a). Instead of using the evidence to prove that the plaintiff did not use reasonable care, it is offered to prove that the defendant did use reasonable care. It is not admissible for this purpose either.

(c) This is a common wrong answer. Most testimony is self-serving. Each side offers testimony to strengthen its case. It is not a reason to exclude it.

Before we leave this choice, let me caution you not to dismiss this answer as always wrong. If, for example, the question concerned Hearsay, a self-serving statement would be neither an admission nor a statement against interest, both of which are reasons to admit the testimony. You can see how this choice could be used as a correct one. Always look at the reason why testimony is offered.

(d) By now we know that this choice is correct. Since this is a "because" choice, we also know the reason why it is correct.

In this question, the correct choice states why choices (a) and (b) are wrong. Choice (d) speaks of the evidence not pertaining to Pam's fall. Both (a) and (b) refer to due care in the past. Because the floor was safe a week, month, year, or minute before Pam fell does not mean it was safe when she fell.

Let's take a follow-up question:

# EXAMPLE:

If Pam offered to prove that the day after she fell Olga had the tile taken up and replaced with a new floor covering, the trial judge should rule the evidence:

    (a) Admissible, because it is relevant to the issue of whether Olga retained control of the entrance.

    (b) Admissible, because it shows that Olga knew of the unsafe condition of the entrance when Pam fell.

    (c) Inadmissible, because there was no evidence that the new floor covering would be any safer than the old.

    (d) Inadmissible, as against public policy of making repairs to prevent further injury regardless of fault.

 Answer the question before reading the explanation that follows.

Let's reverse the order on this one.

(**d**) Abstractly, this is true. Whenever we see a true statement, we can't dismiss it. However, we know that evidence questions are loaded with true statements. It's usually the purpose for which the evidence it offered that determines if the statement applies to this case. Let's reserve judgment on this choice.

(**c**) The importance of this choice is how fast you dismissed it. If you took more than a few seconds to dismiss it, you need more practice. It's thinking about a choice like this for ten or more seconds that can cause you to run short of time on the exam.

Sometimes when a choice makes no sense, you start looking for the hidden meaning. As mentioned before, the examiners will give you lots of nonsense answers. You should recognize one like this by now and waste no time on it.

(b) This is a false statement. Fixing the floor after the fall shows awareness of the condition after the fall. It does not show awareness of the condition before or at the time of the fall. Besides, we know that admission for this purpose is against public policy, as explained in choice (d).

(a) This choice sends us back to the facts. We know that if Olga's defense is that she was not negligent, we could not admit the evidence. However, Olga's defense is that she retained no control of the entrance. To contradict this, the evidence is admissible.

Once we know that this is the purpose of the evidence, we know that the public policy argument does not apply. We can now eliminate choice (d). The only correct choice is (a).

# REAL PROPERTY

You know that Real Property questions can be difficult. Let's look at an easy one. The purpose is to show that sometimes you can get by without in depth knowledge.

## EXAMPLE:

Larry leased property to Lenny for a term of ten years. The lease contained a clause prohibiting Lenny from subletting his interest. Can Lenny assign his interest under the lease?

   (a) Yes, because restraints on alienation of land are strictly construed.

   (b) Yes, because restraints on alienation are invalid.

   (c) No, because the term subletting includes assignment when the term is employed in a lease.

   (d) No, because even in the absence of an express prohibition on assignment, a tenant may not assign without the landlord's permission.

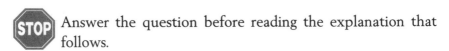 Answer the question before reading the explanation that follows.

**(a)** This question can be answered if you know the general concept. The law allows restraints of subletting and assignment, but does not favor them. If you know this, you know a court would not prohibit assignment unless the lease specifically stated the prohibition. Since this lease does not specifically prohibit assignment, you know that Lenny can assign. Therefore, you know this choice is possibly correct, even if you're not quite sure what it means.

**(b)** Again, you know the general rule that restraints are allowed if specifically stated. In other words, they're not always invalid, as this choice states.

(c)You know that subletting and assignment are different. Assignment is not a type of subletting, as this choice states.

(d) This goes against our general rule. If the law does not favor these restraints, it would not presume them when not present in the lease.

You can see that sometimes even a very general knowledge of the subject matter may be enough to get you to the right choice. Here the general knowledge that the law allows these prohibitions, but does not favor them, is adequate to think your way through to the correct choice.

Let's try a more difficult one.

# EXAMPLE:

Green conveys Blackacre to White using the following words: "To White, his heirs and assigns, but if Blue is still alive 22 years from today, to Blue, his heirs and assigns." The conveyance is:

    (a) Valid, because Blue's interest is a reversion.

    (b) Valid, because Blue's interest must vest, if at all, within a life in being plus 21 years.

    (c) Invalid, both as to White and Blue.

    (d) Invalid, as it violates the Rule Against Perpetuities.

**STOP** Answer the question before reading the explanation that follows.

**(a)** This is simply an incorrect definition. A reversion would be back to Green.

**(b)** The facts state that Blue is currently alive and must stay alive to get the property. This means that the property must vest in Blue within a life in being (Blue's). The 22 years is not relevant. It could be one year and have the same significance.

**(c)** Even if you don't know the Rule Against Perpetuities, you know that there's nothing wrong with the conveyance to White. This makes choice (c) wrong even if the rule is violated. If the rule were violated, the property would go to White.

**(d)** Since (b) is right, this choice must be wrong.

You can see that you would have to know the rule to be sure of your answer. However, you could have eliminated choices (a) and (c) without knowing the rule and improved your odds.

# TORTS

Since there are many Negligence questions on the exam, let's use a couple as examples. Let's also omit specific names and frame the question in general terms in order to concentrate on the choices rather than the facts.

## EXAMPLE:

Plaintiff is lying drunk in a field near the road. Defendant, a passing motorist and stranger to Plaintiff, sees Plaintiff. He stops his car and looks closely at Plaintiff. He decides not to aid Plaintiff and leaves. Later another motorist negligently runs off the road and injures Plaintiff. Will Plaintiff win a suit against Defendant for negligence for failure to aid Plaintiff?

 (a) Yes, because by stopping, Defendant assumed a duty to aid Plaintiff.

 (b) Yes, because Defendant caused Plaintiff's injuries by failing to aid Plaintiff.

 (c) No, if Defendant in no way made the situation worse than it already was.

 (d) No, because Plaintiff created the risk of harm by getting drunk.

 Answer the question before reading the explanation that follows.

(a) This is not correct law. Stranger's don't have or create a duty to aid someone by stopping and looking at him. This should be easy to eliminate.

(b) This is incomplete. Even if you could argue causation, the absence of Duty would still be there. You need all the elements.

(c) This sounds okay. If (d) can be eliminated, this is your answer.

(d) This is wrong for two reasons. First, if Defendant had worsened Plaintiff's, injuries, Defendant could be liable. Second, this would be a defense. You don't use a defense until you establish a Prima Facia case.

Let's take this a step further:

## EXAMPLE:

Plaintiff sues the motorist (we'll call him Driver) who injured him. The theory is again Negligence. The choices are:

(a) Yes, because Driver negligently injured Plaintiff.

(b) Yes, because Plaintiff was in a helpless condition.

(c) No, because Driver didn't see Plaintiff before hitting him.

(d) No, because Plaintiff's intoxication in fact caused his injuries.

Let's say that this question may have more than one correct choice.

 Answer the question before reading the explanation that follows.

(a) The negligence of Driver caused (actually and proximately) Plaintiff's injuries. You have to pick this one. Are there any more correct ones?

(b) Being in a helpless condition may show an absence of contributory negligence. It certainly does not prove negligence on Driver's part.

(c) This is easy to dismiss. If the theory of the suit required intent to harm Plaintiff, this might be a defense. It does not negate any of the elements of Negligence.

(d) This is not supported by the facts. Driver's hitting Plaintiff with the car caused the injuries. If the injuries were from exposure from lying in the field, this could be correct.

Plaintiff's intoxication might be contributory negligence. Don't confuse that with causation. Causation is part of the plaintiff's case. Contributory negligence is a defense.

You can see that simply going through the elements and then the defenses, and then isolating the choices and not relating them to each other, makes your decision much easier.

Remember, it's not how many sample questions you do that will get you ready to pass the bar exam, it's how many you do properly.

# APPENDIX B:
# STATE EXAM REQUIREMENTS

The following is a list of the requirements of each state for Multistate testing. The Multistate Bar Exam (MBE) is the multiple-choice exam. The Multistate Essay Exam (MEE) is not yet required in most states. The Multistate Professional Responsibility Exam (MPRE) is required by almost as many states as the MBE, and the Multistate Performance Test (MPT) is becoming more popular.

There is controversy as to whether adopting the shorter MEE and MPT "waters down" the exam. California, for example, refuses to shorten their three-day, eighteen-hour exam.

# STATE EXAM REQUIREMENTS

| | MBE | MEE | MPRE | MPT |
|---|---|---|---|---|
| Alabama | Yes | Beginning 7/03 | Yes | Beginning 7/03 |
| Alaska | Yes | | Yes | Yes |
| Arizona | Yes | | Yes | |
| Arkansas | Yes | Yes | Yes | Beginning 7/02 |
| California | Yes | | Yes | |
| Colorado | Yes | | Yes | Yes |
| Connecticut | Yes | | Yes | |
| Delaware | Yes | | Yes | Yes |
| District of Columbia | Yes | Yes | Yes | Yes |
| Florida | Yes | | Yes | |
| Georgia | Yes | | Yes | Yes |
| Guam | Yes | | Yes | Yes |
| Hawaii | Yes | Yes | Yes | Yes |
| Idaho | Yes | Yes | Yes | Yes |
| Illinois | Yes | Yes | Yes | Yes |
| Indiana | Yes | | Yes | Yes |
| Iowa | Yes | | Yes | Yes |
| Kansas | Yes | Yes | Yes | |
| Kentucky | Yes | Yes | Yes | |
| Louisiana | | | Yes | |
| Maine | Yes | | Yes | Yes |
| Maryland | Yes | | | |
| Massachusetts | Yes | | Yes | |
| Michigan | Yes | | Yes | |
| Minnesota | Yes | | Yes | Yes |
| Mississippi | Yes | Yes | Yes | Yes |
| Missouri | Yes | Yes | Yes | Yes |
| Montana | Yes | | Yes | |

|                          | MBE | MEE | MPRE | MPT |
|--------------------------|-----|-----|------|-----|
| Nebraska                 | Yes | Yes | Yes  |     |
| Nevada                   | Yes |     | Yes  | Yes |
| New Hampshire            | Yes |     | Yes  |     |
| New Jersey               | Yes |     | Yes  | Yes |
| New Mexico               | Yes |     | Yes  | Yes |
| New York                 | Yes |     | Yes  | Yes |
| North Carolina           | Yes |     | Yes  |     |
| North Dakota             | Yes | Yes | Yes  | Yes |
| Northern Mariana Islands | Yes |     | Yes  | Yes |
| Ohio                     | Yes |     | Yes  | Yes |
| Oklahoma                 | Yes |     | Yes  |     |
| Oregon                   | Yes |     | Yes  | Yes |
| Pennsylvania             | Yes |     | Yes  | Yes |
| Puerto Rico              |     |     |      |     |
| Republic of Palau        | Yes |     | Yes  |     |
| Rhode Island             | Yes |     | Yes  |     |
| South Carolina           | Yes |     | Yes  |     |
| South Dakota             | Yes | Yes | Yes  | Yes |
| Tennessee                | Yes |     | Yes  |     |
| Texas                    | Yes |     | Yes  | Yes |
| Utah                     | Yes | Yes | Yes  |     |
| Vermont                  | Yes |     | Yes  |     |
| Virgin Islands           | Yes |     | Yes  |     |
| Virginia                 | Yes |     | Yes  |     |
| Washington               |     |     |      |     |
| West Virginia            | Yes | Yes | Yes  | Yes |
| Wisconsin                | Yes |     |      |     |
| Wyoming                  | Yes |     | Yes  |     |

# INDEX

correct choice, 3
marking the answer, 28-29
paragraph answer, 4-5, 28, 29, 76
reading the question, 27-28
Roman numeral, 5, 29, 33, 52, 76
series, 5-6
worst answer, 6
multistate essay examination, 13, 87-96
multistate performance test, 1, 13, 99-105
answers, 101-103
questions, 100
studying, 103

## N

National Conference of Bar Examiners, 8, 38, 88, 99
negligence, 22, 23, 24, 31, 32, 63, 64, 65
comparative, 65
contributory, 22, 25, 65

## P

practice, 15, 29, 36, 38-39, 48

## R

rule against perpetuities, 83, 84

## S

scoring the test, 7, 8
shortening the test, 46-47
skipping questions, 44-47, 49
specific performance, 89
speed, 43-44, 59-60
speed reading, 60

stress, 107-110, 114
strict liability, 27
studying, 11, 14, 15, 16, 25, 29, 31-49, 70, 75, 82, 85, 103, 113, 114
subjects, 3, 63-85
common law, 20
constitutional law, 3, 75-77
contracts, 3, 32, 39, 52, 53, 54, 71-74
criminal law and procedure, 3, 66-71, 72, 75
evidence, 3, 4, 12, 41, 70, 77-82
best evidence, 81
real property, 3, 20, 46, 63, 75, 82, 82-84
torts, 3, 21, 63-65, 70, 71, 72, 75

## T

teaching approach, 55, 56
techniques, 27-29
time restrictions, 2, 43, 44, 45
timers, 15, 36, 38
transportation, 107, 110

## W

warm-up, 48, 49, 108, 110
wrong answers, 32-34, 37-38, 114

# SPHINX® PUBLISHING'S STATE TITLES
### *Up-to-Date for Your State*

## CALIFORNIA

| | |
|---|---|
| CA Power of Attorney Handbook (2E) | $18.95 |
| How to File for Divorce in CA (3E) | $26.95 |
| How to Make a CA Will | $16.95 |
| How to Probate and Settle an Estate in CA | $26.95 |
| How to Start a Business in CA | $18.95 |
| How to Win in Small Claims Court in CA | $16.95 |
| Landlords' Rights and Duties in CA | $21.95 |

## FLORIDA

| | |
|---|---|
| Florida Power of Attorney Handbook (2E) | $16.95 |
| How to File for Divorce in FL (7E) | $26.95 |
| How to Form a Corporation in FL (5E) | $24.95 |
| How to Form a Limited Liability Company in FL | $22.95 |
| How to Form a Partnership in FL | $22.95 |
| How to Make a FL Will (6E) | $16.95 |
| How to Modify Your FL Divorce Judgement (4E) | $24.95 |
| How to Probate and Settle an Estate in FL (4E) | $26.95 |
| How to Start a Business in FL (5E) | $16.95 |
| How to Win in Small Claims Court in FL (6E) | $16.95 |
| Landlords' Rights and Duties in FL (8E) | $21.95 |

## GEORGIA

| | |
|---|---|
| How to File for Divorce in GA (4E) | $21.95 |
| How to Make a GA Will (4E) | $21.95 |
| How to Start a Business in GA (2E) | $16.95 |

## ILLINOIS

| | |
|---|---|
| How to File for Divorce in IL (2E) | $21.95 |
| How to Make an IL Will (3E) | $16.95 |
| How to Start a Business in IL (2E) | $18.95 |
| Landlords' Rights & Duties in IL | $21.95 |

## MASSACHUSETTS

| | |
|---|---|
| How to File for Divorce in MA (3E) | $24.95 |
| How to Form a Corporation in MA | $24.95 |
| How to Make a MA Will (2E) | $16.95 |
| How to Start a Business in MA (2E) | $18.95 |
| The Landlord's Legal Guide in MA | $24.95 |

## MICHIGAN

| | |
|---|---|
| How to File for Divorce in MI (2E) | $21.95 |
| How to Make a MI Will (3E) | $16.95 |
| How to Start a Business in MI (3E) | $18.95 |

*Sphinx Publishing's Legal Survival Guides are directly available from the publisher, or from your local bookstores.*

## Minnesota

| | |
|---|---|
| How to File for Divorce in MN | $21.95 |
| How to Form a Corporation in MN | $24.95 |
| How to Make a MN Will (2E) | $16.95 |

## New York

| | |
|---|---|
| How to File for Divorce in NY (2E) | $26.95 |
| How to Form a Corporation in NY | $24.95 |
| How to Make a NY Will (2E) | $16.95 |
| How to Start a Business in NY | $18.95 |
| How to Win in Small Claims Court in NY | $16.95 |
| Landlords' Rights and Duties in NY | $21.95 |
| New York Power of Attorney Handbook | $19.95 |
| Tenants' Rights in NY | $21.95 |

## North Carolina

| | |
|---|---|
| How to File for Divorce in NC (3E) | $22.95 |
| How to Make a NC Will (3E) | $16.95 |
| How to Start a Business in NC (3E) | $18.95 |
| Landlords' Rights & Duties in NC | $21.95 |

## Ohio

| | |
|---|---|
| How to File for Divorce in OH, 2E | $24.95 |
| How to Form a Corporation in OH | $24.95 |
| How to Make an OH Will | $16.95 |

## Pennsylvania

| | |
|---|---|
| How to File for Divorce in PA (3E) | $26.95 |
| How to Make a PA Will (2E) | $16.95 |
| How to Start a Business in PA (2E) | $18.95 |
| Landlords' Rights and Duties in PA | $19.95 |

## Texas

| | |
|---|---|
| Child Custody, Visitation, and Support in TX | $22.95 |
| How to File for Divorce in TX (3E) | $24.95 |
| How to Form a Corporation in TX (2E) | $24.95 |
| How to Make a TX Will (2E) | $16.95 |
| How to Probate an Estate in TX (2E) | $22.95 |
| How to Start a Business in TX (2E) | $18.95 |
| How to Win in Small Claims Court in TX (2E) | $16.95 |
| Landlords' Rights and Duties in TX (2E) | $21.95 |

*For credit card orders call 1–800–432-7444,*
*write P.O. Box 4410, Naperville, IL 60567-4410, or fax 630-961-2168*

# SPHINX® PUBLISHING ORDER FORM

| BILL TO: | | | SHIP TO: | | |
|---|---|---|---|---|---|
| | | | | | |
| | | | | | |
| Phone # | | Terms | F.O.B. Chicago, IL | | Ship Date |

**Charge my:** ☐ VISA  ☐ MasterCard  ☐ American Express   ☐ **Money Order or Personal Check**

| | | | | | | | | | | | | | | | | | | | | | | | |
|--|--|--|--|--|--|--|--|--|--|--|--|--|--|--|--|--|--|--|--|--|--|--|--|

**Credit Card Number**                                                                 **Expiration Date**

| Qty | ISBN | Title | Retail | Qty | ISBN | Title | Retail |
|---|---|---|---|---|---|---|---|
| | | **SPHINX PUBLISHING NATIONAL TITLES** | | _____ | 1-57248-186-2 | Manual de Beneficios para el Seguro Social | $18.95 |
| _____ | 1-57248-148-X | Cómo Hacer su Propio Testamento | $16.95 | _____ | 1-57248-220-6 | Mastering the MBE | $16.95 |
| _____ | 1-57248-147-1 | Cómo Solicitar su Propio Divorcio | $24.95 | _____ | 1-57248-167-6 | Most Valuable Bus. Legal Forms You'll Ever Need (3E) | $21.95 |
| _____ | 1-57248-166-8 | The Complete Book of Corporate Forms | $24.95 | _____ | 1-57248-130-7 | Most Valuable Personal Legal Forms You'll Ever Need | $24.95 |
| _____ | 1-57248-163-3 | Crime Victim's Guide to Justice (2E) | $21.95 | _____ | 1-57248-098-X | The Nanny and Domestic Help Legal Kit | $22.95 |
| _____ | 1-57248-159-5 | Essential Guide to Real Estate Contracts | $18.95 | _____ | 1-57248-089-0 | Neighbor v. Neighbor (2E) | $16.95 |
| _____ | 1-57248-160-9 | Essential Guide to Real Estate Leases | $18.95 | _____ | 1-57071-348-0 | The Power of Attorney Handbook (3E) | $19.95 |
| _____ | 1-57248-139-0 | Grandparents' Rights (3E) | $24.95 | _____ | 1-57248-149-8 | Repair Your Own Credit and Deal with Debt | $18.95 |
| _____ | 1-57248-188-9 | Guia de Inmigración a Estados Unidos (3E) | $24.95 | _____ | 1-57248-168-4 | The Social Security Benefits Handbook (3E) | $18.95 |
| _____ | 1-57248-187-0 | Guia de Justicia para Victimas del Crimen | $21.95 | _____ | 1-57071-399-5 | Unmarried Parents' Rights | $19.95 |
| _____ | 1-57248-103-X | Help Your Lawyer Win Your Case (2E) | $14.95 | _____ | 1-57071-354-5 | U.S.A. Immigration Guide (3E) | $19.95 |
| _____ | 1-57248-164-1 | How to Buy a Condominium or Townhome (2E) | $19.95 | _____ | 1-57248-138-2 | Winning Your Personal Injury Claim (2E) | $24.95 |
| _____ | 1-57248-191-9 | How to File Your Own Bankruptcy (5E) | $21.95 | _____ | 1-57248-162-5 | Your Right to Child Custody, Visitation, and Support (2E) | $24.95 |
| _____ | 1-57248-132-3 | How to File Your Own Divorce (4E) | $24.95 | _____ | 1-57248-157-9 | Your Rights When You Owe Too Much | $16.95 |
| _____ | 1-57248-100-5 | How to Form a DE Corporation from Any State | $24.95 | | | **CALIFORNIA TITLES** | |
| _____ | 1-57248-083-1 | How to Form a Limited Liability Company | $22.95 | _____ | 1-57248-150-1 | CA Power of Attorney Handbook (2E) | $18.95 |
| _____ | 1-57248-099-8 | How to Form a Nonprofit Corporation | $24.95 | _____ | 1-57248-151-X | How to File for Divorce in CA (3E) | $26.95 |
| _____ | 1-57248-133-1 | How to Form Your Own Corporation (3E) | $24.95 | _____ | 1-57071-356-1 | How to Make a CA Will | $16.95 |
| _____ | 1-57071-343-X | How to Form Your Own Partnership | $22.95 | _____ | 1-57248-145-5 | How to Probate and Settle and Estate in CA | $26.95 |
| _____ | 1-57248-119-6 | How to Make Your Own Will  (2E) | $16.95 | _____ | 1-57248-146-3 | How to Start a Business in CA | $18.95 |
| _____ | 1-57248-200-1 | How to Register Your Own Copyright (4E) | $24.95 | _____ | 1-57071-358-8 | How to Win in Small Claims Court in CA | $16.95 |
| _____ | 1-57248-104-8 | How to Register Your Own Trademark (3E) | $21.95 | _____ | 1-57071-359-6 | Landlords' Rights and Duties in CA | $21.95 |
| _____ | 1-57071-349-9 | How to Win Your Unemployment Compensation Claim | $21.95 | | | **FLORIDA TITLES** | |
| _____ | 1-57248-118-8 | How to Write Your Own Living Will (2E) | $16.95 | _____ | 1-57071-363-4 | Florida Power of Attorney Handbook (2E) | $16.95 |
| _____ | 1-57248-156-0 | How to Write Your Own Premarital Agreement (3E) | $24.95 | _____ | 1-57248-176-5 | How to File for Divorce in FL (7E) | $26.95 |
| _____ | 1-57248-158-7 | Incorporate in Nevada from Any State | $24.95 | _____ | 1-57248-177-3 | How to Form a Corporation in FL (5E) | $24.95 |
| _____ | 1-57071-333-2 | Jurors' Rights (2E) | $12.95 | _____ | 1-57248-086-6 | How to Form a Limited Liability Co. in FL | $22.95 |
| _____ | 1-57071-400-2 | Legal Research Made Easy (2E) | $16.95 | _____ | 1-57071-401-0 | How to Form a Partnership in FL | $22.95 |
| _____ | 1-57248-165-X | Living Trusts and Other Ways to Avoid Probate (3E) | $24.95 | | | *Form Continued on Following Page*     **Subtotal** _____ | |

| Qty | ISBN | Title | Retail |
|---|---|---|---|
| | | **FLORIDA TITLES (CONT'D)** | |
| ____ | 1-57248-113-7 | How to Make a FL Will (6E) | $16.95 |
| ____ | 1-57248-088-2 | How to Modify Your FL Divorce Judgment (4E) | $24.95 |
| ____ | 1-57248-144-7 | How to Probate and Settle an Estate in FL (4E) | $26.95 |
| ____ | 1-57248-081-5 | How to Start a Business in FL (5E) | $16.95 |
| ____ | 1-57071-362-6 | How to Win in Small Claims Court in FL (6E) | $16.95 |
| ____ | 1-57248-123-4 | Landlords' Rights and Duties in FL (8E) | $21.95 |
| | | **GEORGIA TITLES** | |
| ____ | 1-57248-137-4 | How to File for Divorce in GA (4E) | $21.95 |
| ____ | 1-57248-180-3 | How to Make a GA Will (4E) | $21.95 |
| ____ | 1-57248-140-4 | How to Start Business in GA (2E) | $16.95 |
| | | **ILLINOIS TITLES** | |
| ____ | 1-57071-405-3 | How to File for Divorce in IL (2E) | $21.95 |
| ____ | 1-57248-170-6 | How to Make an IL Will (3E) | $16.95 |
| ____ | 1-57071-416-9 | How to Start a Business in IL (2E) | $18.95 |
| ____ | 1-57248-078-5 | Landlords' Rights & Duties in IL | $21.95 |
| | | **MASSACHUSETTS TITLES** | |
| ____ | 1-57248-128-5 | How to File for Divorce in MA (3E) | $24.95 |
| ____ | 1-57248-115-3 | How to Form a Corporation in MA | $24.95 |
| ____ | 1-57248-108-0 | How to Make a MA Will (2E) | $16.95 |
| ____ | 1-57248-106-4 | How to Start a Business in MA (2E) | $18.95 |
| ____ | 1-57248-209-5 | The Landlord's Legal Guide in MA | $24.95 |
| | | **MICHIGAN TITLES** | |
| ____ | 1-57071-409-6 | How to File for Divorce in MI (2E) | $21.95 |
| ____ | 1-57248-182-X | How to Make a MI Will (3E) | $16.95 |
| ____ | 1-57248-183-8 | How to Start a Business in MI (3E) | $18.95 |
| | | **MINNESOTA TITLES** | |
| ____ | 1-57248-142-0 | How to File for Divorce in MN | $21.95 |
| ____ | 1-57248-179-X | How to Form a Corporation in MN | $24.95 |
| ____ | 1-57248-178-1 | How to Make a MN Will (2E) | $16.95 |
| | | **NEW YORK TITLES** | |
| ____ | 1-57248-141-2 | How to File for Divorce in NY (2E) | $26.95 |
| ____ | 1-57248-105-6 | How to Form a Corporation in NY | $24.95 |
| ____ | 1-57248-095-5 | How to Make a NY Will (2E) | $16.95 |
| ____ | 1-57071-185-2 | How to Start a Business in NY | $18.95 |

| Qty | ISBN | Title | Retail |
|---|---|---|---|
| ____ | 1-57071-187-9 | How to Win in Small Claims Court in NY | $16.95 |
| ____ | 1-57071-186-0 | Landlords' Rights and Duties in NY | $21.95 |
| ____ | 1-57071-188-7 | New York Power of Attorney Handbook | $19.95 |
| ____ | 1-57248-122-6 | Tenants' Rights in New York | $21.95 |
| | | **NORTH CAROLINA TITLES** | |
| ____ | 1-57248-185-4 | How to File for Divorce in NC (3E) | $22.95 |
| ____ | 1-57248-129-3 | How to Make a NC Will (3E) | $16.95 |
| ____ | 1-57248-184-6 | How to Start a Business in NC (3E) | $18.95 |
| ____ | 1-57248-091-2 | Landlords' Rights & Duties in NC | $21.95 |
| | | **OHIO TITLES** | |
| ____ | 1-57248-190-0 | How to File for Divorce in OH (2E) | $24.95 |
| ____ | 1-57248-174-9 | How to Form a Corporation in OH | $24.95 |
| ____ | 1-57248-173-0 | How to Make an OH Will | $16.95 |
| | | **PENNSYLVANIA TITLES** | |
| ____ | 1-57248-211-7 | How to File for Divorce in PA (3E) | $26.95 |
| ____ | 1-57248-094-7 | How to Make a PA Will (2E) | $16.95 |
| ____ | 1-57248-112-9 | How to Start a Business in PA (2E) | $18.95 |
| ____ | 1-57071-179-8 | Landlords' Rights and Duties in PA | $19.95 |
| | | **TEXAS TITLES** | |
| ____ | 1-57248-171-4 | Child Custody, Visitation, and Support in TX | $22.95 |
| ____ | 1-57248-172-2 | How to File for Divorce in TX (3E) | $24.95 |
| ____ | 1-57248-114-5 | How to Form a Corporation in TX (2E) | $24.95 |
| ____ | 1-57071-417-7 | How to Make a TX Will (2E) | $16.95 |
| ____ | 1-57071-418-5 | How to Probate an Estate in TX (2E) | $22.95 |
| ____ | 1-57071-365-0 | How to Start a Business in TX (2E) | $18.95 |
| ____ | 1-57248-111-0 | How to Win in Small Claims Court in TX (2E) | $16.95 |
| ____ | 1-57248-110-2 | Landlords' Rights and Duties in TX (2E) | $21.95 |

**SUBTOTAL THIS PAGE** _____

**SUBTOTAL PREVIOUS PAGE** _____

Shipping — $5.00 for 1st book, $1.00 each additional _____

Illinois residents add 6.75% sales tax _____

Connecticut residents add 6.00% sales tax _____

**TOTAL** _____